Feminism(s) on the Edge
of the Millennium
Rethinking Foundations and Future Debates

Edited by
Krista Hunt
and
Christine Saulnier

Inanna Publications and Education Inc.
Toronto, Ontario

Published by:
Inanna Publications and Education Inc.
operating as *Canadian Woman Studies/les cahiers de la femme*
212 Founders College, York University
4700 Keele Street
Toronto, Ontario M3J 1P3
Telephone: (416) 736-5356 Fax (416) 736-5765
Email: cws/cf @yorku.ca Web site: www.yorku.ca/cwscf

Printed and Bound in Canada
by University of Toronto Press, Inc.

Cover Design/Interior Design: Luciana Ricciutelli
Cover Art: Rosita Johanson
"The Dream," Thread Painting, 11.5" x 11.5"

National Library of Canada Cataloguing in Publication Data
Main entry under title:
Feminism(s) on the edge of the millennium:
rethinking foundations and future debates

ISBN 0-9681290-5-6

1. Feminist theory. I. Hunt, Krista, 1974–
II. Saulnier, Christine, 1970–

HQ1190.F46 2001   305.42'01   C2001-930398-X

Contents

Section I:
Deconstructing Binaries

Section II:
Contesting Foundations

Section III:
Rethinking Feminist Politics

Feminism(s) on the Edge of the Millennium

Rethinking Foundations and Future Debates

Acknowledgements

This project was inspired by the hard work and dedication of feminist graduate students who have organized and participated in the Annual Interdisciplinary Feminist Graduate Colloquium at York University over the past twelve years. We would like to extend our commendations to all of the co-ordinators of the colloquium and to recognize their commitment to feminist scholarship and to building a feminist community at York University and beyond. We embarked on this project in the hope that it would serve as a retrospective on the colloquium and encourage similar projects in the future.

We would like to acknowledge the support of the departments, divisions, faculties, research centres, and associations at York University that have made the Colloquium and this book possible. In addition, we would like to thank the administrators at the Faculty of Graduate Studies who have assisted the colloquium organizers with bookkeeping and other administrative tasks.

Thanks also to all of the contributors whose work is featured in this collection. Your enthusiasm for this project from the outset ensured high quality scholarship. We hope we will have the opportunity to collaborate again and look forward to meeting all of the contributors face-to-face to celebrate the completion of this project.

This collection would not have been possible without the warmth, hard work and dedication of Luciana Ricciutelli, the Editor/Managing Editor of Inanna Publications and Education Inc. (operating as *Canadian Woman Studies/les cahiers de la femme*). Thank you for making our first editorial experience a rewarding one. As well, we appreciate the experienced advice of Fran Beer and the rest of the *Canadian Woman Studies* board, and are grateful for their support of this project.

We want to thank our experienced colleague and faculty advisor Leah Vosko for her editorial assistance and professional advice. We also want to extend our thanks to Melanie Stewart Millar who was an indispensable sounding-board throughout this process. To both Leah and Melanie, thank you for your friendship, and for always exceeding collegial obligations.

We especially want to thank our family and friends who encouraged us from the start. To our partners, Michael Alex and Michel Gallant, thank you for your support and insistence that we persevere through the challenges we encountered. Thanks for patiently sitting through "dinner meetings," reminding us that we were friends before editors, and advising us to take occasional, but necessary, breaks.

Last but not least, we want to thank each other for the collaborative, supportive friendship which continues to nurture these kinds of projects. We have learned that working collaboratively requires honesty, openness, and flexibility, qualities which serve to enhance these types of projects. While collaborative projects are more rare in the academy, this work demands the development of unique skills which are essential to both teaching and learning. That such a creative project like this collection was made possible, inspires us to search for more opportunities to work together and with other feminists in and beyond the university-setting.

Introduction

Challenges on the Edge:
Feminism(s) in the New Millennium

Krista Hunt and Christine Saulnier

Over the years, feminists have struggled to create spaces within and across academic disciplines for graduate students to pursue feminist studies. However, the pressure of "external" forces such as globalization and economic restructuring intensifies our struggle just to maintain these spaces, let alone to create new spaces for feminist scholarship to flourish. In this neoliberal era, the public sector has come under attack. Universities are under pressure to manage their resources more efficiently, while producing graduates that will strengthen the country's so-called global competitive edge and advance the "knowledge-economy" in Canada. In response to these pressures and to new labour market demands, university administrations are reallocating their research and teaching resources away from Liberal Arts (where feminism has made the most impact) to "applied" programs such as technology and business. The rationalization of post-secondary education has particular implications for the feminist spaces created within universities. While feminist scholarship has been tolerated since the 1970s, feminists continue to encounter resistance in traditional departments, as well as limited access to graduate Women's Studies programmes.[1] Under neoliberalism, however, the legitimacy of feminist courses, research, and pedagogy are becoming increasingly vulnerable.

The nature of the moment we are living in, characterized by a process of increased trade, rapid technological change, increased cross-border financial flows, capital mobility, and cultural transfers, calls into question feminist knowledge production—as well as the political sites from which feminists think, write, and act. The foundations of the past have been established based on geographical, historical, cultural, and other boundaries. However, the shifting boundaries, whether public/private, international/national or state/market, undermine the assumptions and sites of contemporary feminist politics (Brodie 1994: 46). The challenge for feminists then is to negotiate the dynamism of politics, by continuing to reassess theoretical tenets and to redefine political struggles in order to push this movement forward.

Besides these "external" pressures, the foundations of feminist politics are challenged by "internal" debates as women's different social, political, cultural, and sexual realities, among others are finally acknowledged. Feminism has been critiqued for ignoring the differences between women,[2] not only causing marginalization but also creating a hierarchy of oppression. As Audre Lorde argues, differences—be they race, age or sex—are real and must be recognized. She states that "it is not those differences that are separating us. It is rather our refusal to recognize those differences and to examine the distortions that result from our misnaming them and their effects upon human behaviour and expectations" (1997: 375). In recognizing the differences between women, no one site of oppression can be given primacy. In response, new schools of feminist thought have developed that appear to be in conflict with earlier ones, particularly as they raise questions about universalizing ideas of "sameness" (such as those evoked by "sisterhood").

Schools of thought—new and old—and the reality of women's different needs and experiences have left some feminists with the feeling that working toward common feminist goals is impossible. Whether we can or want to, even in principle, define a cohesive feminist movement may be the most important question facing feminists in the new millennium. That many feminists are preoccupied with this question perhaps points to both the major challenge facing feminists and to our common goal: how to remain committed to collective action to improve the status of women, while rejecting simple solutions and universal assumptions. However, as Valerie Bryson warned in her assessment of the future for feminist theory in the 1990s, we must ensure that we do not confuse "particular solutions with universal goals" (1992: 263). Fighting against the multiplicity of complex factors (interests, ideas, and institutions) that work against social justice, means feminism must be flexible, plural and most importantly strategic if it is to avoid becoming an elite inward-looking activity. Heeding Bryson's warning means that when feminists assess priorities and possibilities for change, they must think, write, and act in ways that enable them to make effective political choices.

Feminist Graduate Students on the Edge

Feminism(s) on the Edge of the Millennium reflects this particular historical moment in which these feminist graduate students think, write, and act. What we share is our commitment to developing theories and conducting research that captures the multiplicity and interconnectedness of political power relations which work to oppress different groups of women. As editors of this volume, we take advantage of this moment to reflect on achievements and past struggles, and to consider another century of challenges, opportunities, and victories. This collection does not represent any one feminism, but an array of feminist theories that draw on liberal, radical, socialist, post-colonial, and postmodern feminism, among other feminist and non-feminist bodies of knowledge. While we want to stress the diversity of perspectives within feminist thought, it is clear from this collection that our work is connected by our commitment to addressing the effects of gender-based oppression in its various manifestations.

Feminism(s) on the Edge of the Millennium showcases the work of graduate students which has been presented at the Interdisciplinary Feminist Graduate Colloquium at York University. Through this work, these students have contributed to feminist debates. This book focuses on current issues which occupy public debates, and theoretical works that contribute to developing "new" feminist theory. The authors in this volume are on the epistemological cutting edge, offering insights that can further social and political action and/ or contribute to academic work. This collection will therefore be of interest to students and faculty working on feminist issues, those working in government, and anyone interested in issues related to the Internet, domestic technologies, health policy, neoliberal restructuring, racism, violence against women, and reproduction, to name a few.

Each author in this collection offers recommendations and cautions that feminists and others should consider incorporating into their work. In an era that is characterized by rapid technological change, Melanie Stewart Millar challenges feminists to think about what more and more technologies in the home may mean for the power relations there. She reminds us that feminists have successfully made visible other politics masked by capitalist (consumerist) impulses such as the politics of domestic technologies. For her part, Joanne Wright leaves feminists with a project: articulating women's experiences of birth and pregnancy to further our understanding of the multiple, historical, and cultural meanings of reproduction. Similarly, Chris Klassen challenges us to reconsider feminist spirituality in light of feminist deconstructions of sex and gender. Michelle Lowry calls on feminists (especially those who are white) to adopt an anti-racist politics struggling against different forms of oppression while relating across them. She argues that it is important that we find new ways to understand cultural differences and thus to relate to each other. Similarly, Debra Langan advises feminists that understanding how to challenge dominant discourses, so as to promote alternative critical ideologies, is a promising line of inquiry for those who want to continue to work toward effecting changes in social relations. She offers us new insights to inform our actions to eradicate violence against women on and off university campuses.

In addition to these insights, the authors in this collection also consider what additional spaces may have opened for active political engagement. Lucy Luccisano sheds light on communal kitchens as an additional political space available to poor women, and Krista Hunt raises important questions about the Internet as a cultural space and a organizational tool. Diane Crocker argues that feminists may have to refocus our energies away from the judicial system unless we can advance a more complex discursive understanding of women's lives when such serious social problems as wife abuse are being judged there. All three authors clearly argue that few spaces are without contradictions and complexities. What Christine Saulnier ultimately argues is that feminists must work so that women are empowered to interpret their own needs according to the complexities of their roles.

What links the contributors to this volume is not only our commitment to feminist theory and research, but also our position on the margins of the academy. To be located on the edge of the academy is both a position of marginality and a particular vantage point from which to critique the academy and strive to improve it. Feminists remain "on the edge" of the academy in terms of numbers, representation in traditional departments, and as full professors and graduate students. Feminist students and teachers often find themselves marginalized within departments, encouraged to redirect their focus to non-feminist issues, or pressured to only do their work in Women's Studies programs. When we focus on gender relations, we are accused of narrowing our area of expertise, thus threatening our employability. Finally, we are "on the edge" in academia because the very nature of the critical work that we do is threatening. It is through this position of marginality that we must fight to maintain past gains and look forward to new challenges. As such, this collection is "on the edge" because graduate students are arguably the most cutting-edge academics; the result of their exposure to the newest debates, their passion and enthusiasm, their commitment to challenging the status quo, and their desire to set a new agenda.

From alternative classrooms to alternative conferences, feminists have redefined the way the academy can operate by fostering inclusive, open, and positive spaces for people to learn. We have challenged the chilly climate, discrimination in hiring, and sexual harassment, and we continue to struggle on these grounds. For many feminists scattered throughout the university, it is essential to create networks that disciplines and departments often fail to provide. It is through these networks that feminist students discover scholars familiar with their research and most able to provide constructive criticism, and solicit advice on which courses to take and which professors to seek out for supervision. These networks also foster opportunities to present and publish their work, such as this book inspired by the Interdisciplinary Feminist Graduate Colloquium.

Over the past twelve years, this Interdisciplinary Feminist Graduate Colloquium at York University has provided graduate students with an opportunity to present their work to an audience of peers. As graduate students "on the edge" of our careers, collective opportunities—like conferences—help us to gain professional experience. The Colloquium has been instrumental in facilitating contacts among graduate students engaged in feminist studies. At first, it only drew together students from York University, but has since attracted participants from across Ontario. This conference provides a forum for students to share their work across the often artificial and constraining boundaries of the disciplines. Often, feminist students in other disciplines are grappling with the same questions, and our knowledge of different theories makes for important interdisciplinary discussions that serve to enrich our particular perspectives. Not only is the forum important on an intellectual level, it also serves to decrease the isolation that is endemic to the work we do.

The Colloquium has tried to create a collegial and supportive environment most conducive to scholarly exchange. Many participants have remarked that unlike more traditional, disciplinary conferences, the feedback received at the Colloquium is critical, engaged, and productive—the result of presenting to an audience that is familiar with and committed to feminist issues. While this is the strength of an interdisciplinary feminist forum, there are also pitfalls. As one presenter stated, while "the Colloquium's main strength is its ability to bring together feminist scholars throughout the York community ... participants occasionally forget their audience and present papers that may be inaccessible to members of different disciplines, or that do not raise questions or issues with which others can engage."[3] It is our shared commitment to feminist scholarship and our unique, disciplinary perspectives that have worked to create a space to "renew our commitment to feminist work" within and beyond the boundaries of the disciplines.

In the academy, feminists continue to create spaces to network, collaborate, and innovate. As past organizers and presenters at the Interdisciplinary Feminist Graduate Colloquium, we are committed to strengthening this scholarly forum and contributing to its continued success. It is our experience that the Colloquium is one space through which to energize and inspire feminists in the academy—a purpose we hope this collection serves as well.

Outlining *Feminism(s) on the Edge of the Millennium*

The common theme running through all of the papers in this collection is the importance of discourse in producing identities, social relations, and political practices that both maintain and resist traditional power structures. Discourses construct boundaries that include and exclude certain political actors and claims by the way they socially construct what is legitimate. These discourses reinforce "truths" and assign dominant meaning to our experiences, which affect the way feminists mobilize around issues and the way policies are constructed (Phillips 1996). As such, discourses are an important site for feminist struggle.

All the papers within this volume contribute to strengthening new feminist theory and practice by challenging the boundaries created by dominant discourses, thus opening space for alternative conceptualizations of society's problems and solutions. To best reflect this theme, the collection is organized into three sub-themes: Deconstructing Binaries, Contesting Foundations, and Rethinking Feminist Politics. These sub-themes overlap in their desire to straddle divides and understand contradictions. In exploring these themes, we strengthen feminist thought while recognizing the insecurity of grand narratives and universal statements. Under the first theme, Melanie Stewart Millar, Lucy Luccisano, and Christine Saulnier deconstruct binaries as one form of boundary construction. A binary or dualism conceptualizes two entities as fixed, impermeable, dichotomies that create a hierarchical opposition through rigid differentiation. Deconstructing binaries, whether hierarchical or not, unmasks differences, similarities, and links which are necessary to better understand and meet women's needs (Grewal and Kaplan 1994). These authors seek to understand what it would mean if we could mediate such binaries, reconceptualizing them not as oppositional and hierarchical but as creative tensions.

Melanie Stewart Millar explores the public/private as one such dualism in western political thought. She asks a question that all three authors in this section address: does deconstructing the public/private category or any other dualism help feminists respond to women's needs? To answer this question Stewart Millar considers the impact of domestic technologies on our dualistic thinking about the public and private and specifically on the "mechanics of domestic power."

Like Stewart Millar, Lucy Luccisano explores the limitations of binary conceptualizations of poor women's struggles in Peru and Mexico. She challenges the dualistic conceptualization of the public/private, personal/political and practical/strategic gender interests for understanding how communal kitchens are politicized public spaces that challenge gendered boundaries and power configurations in personal relationships. She considers how isolated experiences hidden within the home can become collective activities once domestic responsibilities are no longer private. Luccisano explores whether such activities contribute to the politicization of everyday life or whether establishing community kitchens is a means of off-loading state responsibilities onto women in the management of their own social needs.

Christine Saulnier examines the state as employer and the grounds upon which nursing organizations contest health system restructuring in New Brunswick, Canada. She too challenges the dualistic classification of nurses' strategies as solving practical or strategic gender interests and as using problem-solving or critical-thinking approaches. Saulnier grounds her analysis of the nursing organizations' strategic dilemmas in their contradictory position as professional workers and as caregivers. Complementing the contributions of Luccisano and Stewart Millar, she seeks to understand whether neoliberal restructuring offers women opportunities for advancing their needs or whether the dominant ideologies and government agendas foreclose such possibilities.

Under the second theme, "Contesting Foundations," Chris Klassen, Debra Langan, and Joanne Wright contest the foundational assumptions that underpin dominant discourses. According to Chris Klassen, for many women feminist spirituality is becoming an important part of their identities. As such, feminists must examine this work in order to analyze its foundational assumptions. In her piece, Klassen critically examines the work of feminist theologian Carol Christ and deconstructs Christ's use of the categories "women" and "female," as well as her limited recognition of the differences between women.

In so doing, Klassen contributes to "unbuilding" problematic underpinnings of feminist religion and leads the way toward "re-building" a kind of feminist spirituality that is attentive to the vast differences between women.

Debra Langan's piece explores how "talk in social interaction contributes to the perpetuation of ideologies around gendered power relations." Her research on undergraduates' views of the chilly climate, sexual harassment, and sexual assault issues, furthers our understanding of how ideologies and discourses work to sustain violence against women on and off campus. By examining not why, but *how* women are victimized, she offers feminists ways to rethink how to work to change "social relations of power which perpetuate and reinforce male violence against women."

Metaphors are often integral to the foundational assumptions underpinning dominant discourses and thus also need to be critically analyzed. In this section, Joanne Wright explores reproductive metaphors and argues that we need to further our understanding of the significance of female reproductive abilities by challenging the way these abilities have been distorted. She does so by examining reproduction in western cultural discourse through an analysis of two contrasting positions offered by Plato and Mary O'Brien: she argues that one fails to do justice to the significance of pregnancy and birth, while the other uncritically celebrates them.

Rethinking feminist politics in ways that capture the creative, contradictory, and complex tensions inherent in political strategies is the focus of the final group of papers. Rethinking feminist politics in regard to western feminist analysis of the Islamic practice of veiling, Michelle Lowry presents an anti-racist, feminist understanding of the veil that negotiates the tensions between sameness and difference and presents a more fluid understanding of identity and culture. In so doing, she also negotiates the tensions between cultural relativists and cultural imperialists in debates about veiling as an Islamic "cultural" "tradition" performed in a western context (Canada).

By examining two nineteenth-century trials in which women were charged with killing their abusive husbands, Diane Crocker reveals the complexities of these cases and the challenges of using archival documents produced by the media and the courts to adequately capture women's experiences. Crocker argues that as feminists strategize for the future, especially when assessing judicial intervention, the contradictions that operate within the court system must be captured and incorporated into our politics.

On the theme of political strategy, Krista Hunt considers the potential of the Internet as a tool for global feminism(s) by negotiating the tensions surrounding identity politics which underlie current efforts at global feminist organizing. In her piece, Hunt examines the problems and possibilities encountered by feminists using the Internet, including issues of access and the struggle to subvert the male-defined, capitalist shape of this space. She examines the ways in which women's groups are using the Internet to organize globally, how these groups negotiate debates about the politics of identity and difference, and how postmodern conceptions of global feminism(s) may provide a basis to re-think identity politics and, importantly, political practice. Of particular importance is her critical discussion of both the pros and cons of using this technology to subvert its dominant tendencies.

Conclusion: Challenges for the New Millennium

By deconstructing binaries, contesting foundations, and rethinking feminist politics the feminists within this collection have, in diverse ways, contributed to challenging dominant discourses in order to practice feminism(s) differently. The authors pose new questions while revisiting old ones, challenge orthodoxy within feminist and non-feminist thought, and examine current ontological, epistemological, and methodological debates. Clearly, it is critical for feminists to address the nuances of life on the edge of the new millennium and to remain committed to political praxis. Like our subject matter, our own visions and perspectives will undoubtedly change, but it is these processes of reflection, debate, and revisioning that will continue to push feminism(s) forward. Through projects like the Colloquium and this collection, feminist graduate students make new contributions to feminist thought. Making effective political choices in the new millennium promises to be as difficult as ever in light of challenges from within and beyond feminism. However, we can gain strength both from the strong feminist legacy of the past and from each other to move our dynamic projects forward.

[1]For a discussion of these issues in detail see Shteir (1996).
[2]For some important critiques see Bannerji (1996); Butler (1990); Calhoun (1997); hooks (1981); Mohanty (1991).
[3]This section draws on our experiences as presenters and organizers of the Colloquium as well as written comments provided to us by past presenters. We asked the presenters to answer four questions: What role do you think the Colloquium plays at York? How has the Colloquium contributed to your

graduate career? What are its strengths and weaknesses? Do you have any recommendations for future Colloquiums? Organizers were also asked the same questions (as most have also been presenters) and additionally were asked: How has the Colloquium changed over the years? and What difficulties did they encounter as organizers? We want to thank all those who responded.

References

Bannerji, Himani. "On the Dark Side of the Nation: Politics of Multiculturalism and the State of 'Canada'." *Journal of Canadian Studies* 31.3 (Fall 1996) 103-128.

Brodie, Janine. "Shifting the Boundaries: Gender and the Politics of Restructuring." *The Strategic Silence*. Ed. Isabella Bakker. London & Ottawa: Zed Books with North-South Institute, 1994.

Bryson, Valerie. *Feminist Political Theory: An Introduction*. London: Macmillan, 1992.

Butler, Judith. *Gender Trouble: Feminism and the Subversion of Identity*. New York/London: Routledge, 1990.

Calhoun, Cheshire. "Separating Lesbian Theory from Feminist Theory." *Feminist Social Thought: A Reader*. Ed. Diana Tietjens Meyers. New York and London: Routledge, 1997. 199-218.

Grewal, Inderpal and Caren Kaplan. Introduction. *Scattered Hegemonies*. Minnesota: Minnesota University press, 1994.

hooks, bell. *Ain't I a Woman*. Boston: South End Press, 1981.

Lorde, Audre. "Age, Race, Class and Sex: Women Redefine Difference," *Dangerous Liaisons: Gender, Nations, and Postcolonial Perspectives*. Eds. Anne McClintock, Aamir Mufti, and Ella Shohat. Minneapolis: University of Minnesota Press, 1997.

Mohanty, Chandra Talpade. "Under Western Eyes: Feminist Scholarship and Colonial Discourses." *Third World Women and the Politics of Feminism*. Eds. Chandra Talpade Mohanty, Ann Russo and Lourdes Torres. Bloomington and Indianapolis: Indiana University Press, 1991. 51-80.

Phillips, Susan D. "Discourse, Identity and Voice: Feminist Contributions to Policy Studies." *Policy Studies in Canada: The State of the Art*. Eds. Laurent Dobuzinskis, Michael Howlett and David Laycock. Toronto: University of Toronto Press, 1996: 242-265.

Shteir, Ann B., Ed. *Graduate Women's Studies: Visions and Realities*. Toronto: Inanna Publications and Education Inc., 1996.

Feminism(s) on the Edge of the Millennium

Section I:
Deconstructing Binaries

Digital Domesticity

Gender, Ideology, and
New Technology in the Home

Melanie Stewart Millar

In her 1999 review of the evolution of western feminist thought, Barbara Arneil argues that "the late 1980s and 1990s have witnessed the emergence of a new third wave of feminism(s)" (1999: 186). One of the most important features of these "new" feminisms is the recognition that the dualistic categories of western political thought, including for example, nature/culture, public/private, reason/passion and so on, must not only be challenged in order to include women, but must themselves be deconstructed. Even the category "woman" itself has been problematized as the universal subject of female emancipation. As a result, much late twentieth-century feminist theory has concerned itself with issues of "identity, difference, particularity and embodiment" (Arneil 1999: 186). As Kemp and Squires note, this theory has also emphasized "the processes of symbolization and representation" over material and sociological concerns (1997: 7). While the theoretical goal of recognizing diversity and transforming existing epistemologies is clearly a worthwhile one, some feminists have cautioned that academic feminism may be becoming less able to offer meaningful resistance to existing power structures and to adequately respond to many of the most pressing issues confronting women today (Kemp and Squires 1997: 13-17).

Meanwhile, beyond the confines of academic journals, conferences, and texts, much of mainstream culture remains untouched by the greater sophistication of new feminist theory. In fact, hegemonic culture continues to perpetuate long-standing dualistic frameworks, whether or not feminists and poststructuralists have deconstructed them. Many of the questions raised by second wave feminists remain unanswered and the revolution they began seems to be fundamentally stalled. While the scope and depth of feminist theory has expanded, we may well question whether we are any closer to resolving many of the basic contradictions and challenges that so many women face in their daily lives. Are we, as feminists, for example, any more able to offer solutions to—or to even entirely understand—the individual struggles of millions of women who, while making inroads into the public sphere, are still primarily responsible for childcare and housework? With the double shift still a reality for so many, has deconstructing the public/private division helped feminists respond to women's needs?[1]

Perhaps these are unfair questions. A lot has changed since the birth of second wave feminism. We are no longer living in the 1970s. We know this because we are surrounded by the symbols of progress. Our homes are littered with high tech communications devices, electronics, and computers. We live in the midst of a new hypermodern consumer culture, surrounded by complexity and the high-speed demands of cell phones, graphic-drenched data, and a globalized multi-media advertising industry. We have become accustomed to rapid technological change and have made an uneasy peace with the giddy mixture of wonder and fear that the digital revolution has come to signify. Rewrapping ourselves in the cellophane wrapper of novelty almost daily, it is sometimes difficult to see ourselves (and our struggles) in the political movements of even a short time ago.

And yet, the return of bell bottoms and crocheted ponchos on the fashion runways is a telling reminder that, as P.T. Anderson notes in his popular 1999 film *Magnolia*, "we may be finished with the past, but the past is not finished with us." In fact, in many ways, the politics and culture of the *fin de millennium* reflect a reassertion of some very traditional beliefs about gender. The last two decades have seen the onset of a period of government economic restructuring that has eroded the welfare state and has had a deeply gendered impact. Many of the social programs receptive to the needs of "working women" have fallen off the public agenda. Despite a widening gendered wage gap, even mild-mannered policies like pay equity have struggled to gain favour.[2] Worldwide, "women are the greatest and fastest growing share of the world's poor" and have actually lost ground as a proportion of the paid labour force since the mid-1980s (Seager 1997: 78, 66). Feminism may be on the edge of the millennium, but many women are still—and increasingly—just living on the edge.

In this neo-conservative political climate, there has also been a marked

increase in regressive discursive and representational messages. North American culture has seen, for example, a return to "family values," the rise of Ally
McBeal as an hysterical and unfulfilled June-Cleaver-wanna-be feminine
icon, and the phenomenal growth of mainstream pseudo-pornographic (and
definitely adolescent) men's magazines like *Maxim*.[3] Meanwhile, our much
lauded "media savvy" has done little to stem the growing tide of eating
disorders or prevent the alarming rise in cosmetic surgeries throughout the
1990s (Seager 1997: 50-51). Contrary to schoolyard wisdom, sticks and stones
are not the only things that hurt; words (and pictures) can too. Even the
growth of the new information technology sector, perhaps *the* symbol of
western progress, has had a deeply ambiguous—if not regressive—impact on
women's opportunities.[4] Far from creating the inclusive cyber-democracy
promised by theorists, the digital economy has, thus far, predominantly
reminded us who counts and who doesn't, who is a one and who is a zero (Sadar
and Ravetz 1996). Almost everywhere we look it would seem, we see more, not
less evidence of dualistic thinking.

In this context, what would it mean to return to one of the fundamental
sites of women's oppression—the home—and assess the changes taking place
there? Will the infusion of more and more technologies into the home (for
purposes other than housework) change the relationship between the public
and private spheres in the future? What if we could learn to understand—even
anticipate—the social construction of domestic spaces and use this critical
knowledge to undermine hegemonic ideologies? Would it be possible to use
the tools of deconstruction to politicize domestic technological consumption—to use theory to disrupt practice? This article provides a preliminary
overview of some of the contemporary relationships between domestic technological consumption and shifting relations of power in the home—what I
call the mechanics of domestic power—as a way of critically engaging with
current waves of technological change and resisting existing inequalities. In so
doing, I will examine some contemporary themes in consumer culture as an
important indicator of ideological change, and explore the need to develop a
new politics of domestic technology.

The Mechanics of Domestic Power

There can be little doubt that within hegemonic western culture, "technology" and "housework" are still two of the most quintessentially gendered
terms. Technology has come to be defined as "what men do" while housework

is "what women do." Technology lives outside the home, in the masculine, paid public sphere, while housework lives inside the home, in the feminine, unpaid private sphere. This rigid dualism has proven highly resistant to change; its status in hegemonic western culture remains largely un-phased by the mechanization of many household tasks, the women's movement, the rise (and fall) of the welfare state, or women's increased presence in the paid labour force. Yet, neither technology nor housework is frequently identified as politically important. It is particularly interesting that despite the fact that computers have entered domestic spaces in droves since the mid 1980s, home computers are not generally seen as "domestic technologies" that interact with other technologies (and people) in the particular, and highly gendered, political space of the home. Rather, the social sciences have predominantly focussed on the effects of digital technology on the labour force outside the home, the possibilities of cyber-democracy, or the construction of new public spaces (and identities) online.[5]

Yet the widespread political and economic significance of computer technology, as well as other domestic technologies, is clear. All technology, particularly the technology that we use to perform the work of sustaining daily life, is intimately involved in the dominant mode of both production *and* reproduction. The market for household conveniences, and the continual re-creation and expansion of this market, fuels the sustenance and growth of appliance and home entertainment industries as well as numerous related utilities, manufacturers, distributors, and retailers. The design, marketing, and distribution of particular domestic technologies also influence dominant perceptions of what constitutes the "good life," how tasks should be structured within the home, and who should perform them. Devices once considered extravagances become necessities, normative notions of cleanliness evolve as new technologies are introduced, and time allocation patterns of different household members change to accommodate appliance functions, cycles, and speeds. New words, values, and leisure activities also enter the culture along with new machines.

The politics of domestic technology do not only operate on a macro-level, characterized by large-scale social and economic change. As Steven Lubar (1998) convincingly argues, one important way that notions of masculinity and femininity are themselves created and recreated on a micro-level is through the use of technologies that themselves embody particular gendered assumptions. Thus, as we learn about various technologies within the gendered environment of the home, we also learn to replicate (or disrupt) traditional power relations of gender. Images of the housewife filling the washing machine with clothes and the male television viewer wired to the remote control help to create normative models of masculine and feminine behaviour. Similarly, as Benston notes, "every time a man repairs the plumbing or a sewing machine while a woman watches, a communication about her helplessness and inferiority is made" (1992: 37). Competency is culturally constructed in complicated ways, especially in the private, domestic sphere; while women are generally viewed as technologically incompetent, men are frequently positioned as domestically incompetent. This creates, for example, the seemingly contradictory cultural depiction of men as both unable to adequately sort laundry according to colour, and exclusively endowed with the ability to design and maintain the most complicated of domestic and industrial technologies.[6]

Existing feminist literature on housework has clearly recognized the significance of household technologies to power relations of gender and of gender ideologies to human interactions with technology. This work predominantly takes one of three forms. First, there are a number of historical studies of women's experience as users of household technologies and as housewives in the domestic sphere.[7] These include studies of rural and urban experience,[8] as well as both narrow studies of highly particularized experience (and technologies) (Busch 1983; Hoy 1985; Kapstein 1981; Rakow 1992), and broad studies that attempt to map the entire history of housework and/or household technology.[9] Second, there are a number of more theoretical and sociological analyses of the relationships between gendered domestic roles, technology used for cooking and housework, and women's political, social, and economic subordination. While historical data remains a component of many of these works, the focus is on gaining a greater theoretical understanding of cooking and housework technologies more generally (Oakley 1974; Luxton 1980). A great deal of this literature has been preoccupied with determining whether housework-related technology has been a boon or bane for women (see Wacjman 1992; Bereano, Bose and Arnold 1985; Bose 1979; Day 1987). While all of this work is very useful, feminist domestic technological inquiry has been almost entirely limited to technologies used for housework and cooking. A more recent, third body of work has begun to politicize the process of consuming and using various household products (including appliances, electronics, and communications devices) and situate consumers as agents in the process of technological change. To this end, a small, but growing body of work is attempting to synthesize existing historical literature on technology,

Melanie Stewart Millar

consumer culture, and social difference.[10] While promising, there remains a need to analyze the full range of domestic technologies, including technologies of housework, yard-work, leisure, and communication, which are socially constructed and marketed in very different ways. By examining a wider range of technologies simultaneously, it may be possible to gain a greater understanding of the complexities of how technologies interact within the home and influence, and are influenced by, hegemonic power relations. This means starting to link historical experience with contemporary realities and future marketing trends in order to define a socially relevant politics of domestic technology for today.

Digital Domesticity

These contemporary realities and trends include a number of recent changes to the social, cultural, and technological composition of the domestic sphere. Canadian census figures suggest that since 1981, there has been a 40 per cent increase in the number of people engaged in paid labour in the home (Menzies 1996: 116). In addition to traditional kinds of paid labour that occur in the home, like domestic cleaning services, childcare and textile piecework, an increasing number of administerial/managerial and clerical jobs are now done in the home (Jackson 1999: D6). Facilitated by the rise of the home computer, and encouraged by the contraction of the welfare state and the growing number of single parent families, more and more women are juggling paid work, housework, and care-giving responsibilities in the home. In fact, between 1981 and 1991, the number of women engaged in paid labour at home grew by 69 percent, compared to 39 percent for men (Hare and Johnson 1999: 31). Much of this new home-based labour is data entry and tele-work—work only made possible through the integration of a variety of technologies previously found only in offices (computers, internet access, fax machines etc.). Service sector jobs also began to invade the home in the 1980s and '90s, as pizza delivery places and assorted consumer information services began having calls re-routed to personnel working in their own homes. How have these changes affected the politics of domestic labour? Have traditional inequalities been challenged or perpetuated by such changes?

The integration of more paid employment into the home does not seem to have challenged the gendered wage gap. Existing studies on female home-based clerical workers indicate annual wages consistently well under $20,000, and repeatedly warn of high stress levels, low job satisfaction and poor working conditions (Menzies 1996: 116). Many women turn to home-work as a means to combine child and/or adult care with paid work. Unfortunately, the low status of such jobs makes them a poor solution to a long-standing problem. The advantages for corporations and governments, however, are clear. Employers can reduce overhead when workers work at home, and may also benefit from the fact that unions have yet to penetrate the domestic work place. Meanwhile, governments can continue to avoid the much-promised, but apparently too costly, "national day care system," if more women combine paid employment with childcare in the home. Such an arrangement is also rhetorically supported by the aforementioned "return to family values" and to "women's place" in the home (Millar 1998; Phizacklea and Wolkowitz 1995; Ocran 1997).

Not surprisingly, perhaps, men's home-based work tends to be in more high status (and high paid) managerial and sales-related fields. Yet men's paid labour in the home has certainly increased, to the point where a new magazine, *Home Office*, appeared in 1997. The magazine provides tips about how to set up a home office, what's new in office equipment, and, not insignificantly, provides advice to men about how to insulate themselves from the demands of domestic life while engaged in paid labour at home. Does the fact that more men are engaging in paid labour in the home mean that more men are participating in unpaid domestic labour at the same time? Unfortunately, studies continue to show that married and common-law men's participation in unpaid household labour (as opposed to childcare) has not changed significantly in the last thirty years (Segal 1990; Kaufman 1999). As we may well have suspected, geographic location is not, it would seem, the fundamental sustaining feature in the public/private divide. How are normative gendered ideas about the roles of men and women in the public and private spheres maintained? Why hasn't the infusion of new technologies into the home helped to facilitate more equitable gender relations?

Many feminists have argued that domestic technological change has not facilitated women's increased participation outside the home as much as it has insulated the unequal power relations of the domestic sphere from change.[11] For example, the microwave oven and assorted convenience foods have reinforced women's responsibility for cooking, despite the contracted time available to perform this task. Daily shower cleansing sprays may be seen as a recent example of a similar phenomenon. In response to women's increasingly demanding lifestyles, a technological solution is offered that is marketed as "labour saving" at the same time as it increases standards of cleanliness and reinforces women's responsibility for domestic jobs. Daily shower cleansing sprays suggest that it is no longer acceptable for the shower to get dirty at all —rather, the idealized female housewife must spray the shower clean on a daily basis.[12]

There can be little doubt that new employment realities have been accompanied by the reassertion of highly gendered domestic discourse. While increasing numbers of men and women have seen their home and workplace conflate, the late 1980s and '90s have also seen dominant white middle class ideology emphasize the desire to "cocoon" in suburban homes equipped with televisions, video cassette recorders, home entertainment systems, video games, home computers, and Internet access. The majority of these home electronics devices have been marketed in a manner that continues to reinforce traditional gender roles, even as they may also serve to dissolve the line between public and private by making the home a more efficient site of entertainment and advertising consumption. Indeed, even the most cursory examination of the advertisers included in men's magazines versus women's magazines clearly indicates the association of masculinity with stereo equipment, vcr's, televisions and personal computers, and the association of femininity with domestic appliances like vacuum cleaners, stoves, dishwashers, and washing machines.[13] My analysis of over three hundred television advertisements for domestic technologies ranging from lawnmowers to blenders to digital devices reveals a similar, highly gendered association.[14] In fact, where male and female characters are shown in advertisements for products not associated with their gender, their presence is explicitly remarkable and used either as a source of humour or fantasy. It would seem that the home continues to be discursively constructed as a man's castle of leisure and a woman's dungeon of drudgery, regardless of whether or not that home is wired to the Internet or is a site of paid labour.

There has also been a recent rise in traditional (if not intensified) forms of domesticity, as Martha Stewart's world of wallpaper-to-towels co-ordination, meticulous pot pourri projects, home-baked exotic breads, and other "good things" grows. In the last twenty years, more and more television shows and magazines have explained how to create complicated "faux finishes" and "window treatments" and cable channels dedicated solely to the creation of domestic bliss have emerged, including House and Garden Television Canada.[15] This reassertion of domesticity is closely linked to the continued construction of heterosexual romance and marriage as a consumer event.[16] Perhaps as an antidote to the high speed world outside the home, domestic scenes are once again in vogue—especially as defined by home designers and advertising executives alike. Recent changes in design reflect an end to the gleaming whiteness of 1980s modernity and a return of traditional "comfort kitchens," purporting to contain "sugar and spices and modern devices," including computer stations (Mumford 1996). Not only do new designs combine high technology with familiar décor, but they also combine a desire for individuality with products from around the globe, sold in transnational magazines throughout the world (Usherwood 1997). This renewed interest in home beautification is all big business, of course. Statistics Canada recently reported that more than $20 billion dollars is spent in home improvement stores in Canada alone (Southex Exhibitions Inc.). The domestic sphere, it would seem, is both in a rapid state of flux and, more simply, just "in."

Directing the Home of the Future: What's Next?

It is difficult to predict where the current intensification of the domestic sphere will lead in the future. Yet some of the dynamics involved are evident in the ways that new domestic technologies are being designed and marketed. For example, in an effort to "debut tomorrow's new products, today," the "high tech home" was introduced to consumers at the 2000 National Home Show by way of 3Com's *Home Connect* and IBM's *Home Director*. The latter promises to enhance the "security, convenience and connectivity" of family life. Providing the "foundation" for the private sphere of the future, *Home Director* coordinates home functions, "making your life easier" by increasing the efficiency of domestic life and facilitating the incorporation of an ever-expanding array of digital home entertainment and communications devices. Aside from the alarming visual display of the IBM logo disappearing into the foundation of a suburban family home, the marketing of *Home Director* provides important insights into the ways that the public and private spheres are being reconfigured through technology. Some of the "features" highlighted in *Home Director*'s promotional video clearly perpetuate traditional gender relations and attempt to extend the hypermodern efficiency of corporate life to the private sphere. A female actor/consumer is told that she can monitor her children playing in another room from the kitchen via surveillance equipment, while her spouse is told that the couple can easily convert bedrooms into home offices or network all the computers in their home. Other features include the coordination of home security systems with lighting and heating systems.

Of course, *Home Director* is not really designed for the mundane task of reducing the thermostat at night or turning lights on and off. This would be rather like using a cruise missile to get rid of a pesky mosquito—a bit too much fire power. Like many new technologies, the *raison d'être* of *Home Director* is hinted at in a single, unobtrusive marketing line: with *Home Director* "you'll be positioned for the explosion of Internet and entertainment products on the horizon." Just as the television industry does not make the bulk of its profits from selling televisions but from selling television audiences to advertisers, *Home Director* may be less about selling a box full of wires than it is about intensifying the process of converting private space into a form of public space that facilitates increasing levels of consumption. The product creates the infrastructure needed for the continued colonization of recreational space by capitalist production and consumption. Homes become more efficient sites for information consumption, provide more opportunities for mediated experience, and structure more and more facets of human life along the lines of either production (via the home office) or consumption (via the home computer and television). The use of traditional gendered imagery may simply make the new technology feel familiar to an uncertain public.[17]

Home Director provides just one example of how domestic technologies are implicated in the complex and highly gendered process of restructuring the public and private spheres. There are many others. Exactly how new developments in domestic technologies may influence (and be influenced by) existing relations of power in the future requires a great deal more study. Unfortunately, our ability to recognize and adequately analyze the politics of domestic technology may well become more, not less difficult in the future. Just as the IBM logo disappeared into the foundations of the home in the *Home Director* promotional video, new domestic technologies are disappearing into the walls of our homes. Consumers are even explicitly advised to preserve that "homey feeling" in their home offices by looking "for ways to keep boxy office electronics, such as fax machines, out of sight" (Cooper 1996: 144). In addition, the politics of domestic technology are in danger of being ignored completely if we fail to recognize the importance of consumption and technological change as political processes that are produced both materially and ideologically.

In the past, feminism has been particularly good at rendering the invisible visible, at seeing beyond the discursive "smoke and mirrors" to the political heart of social relations. We must not allow the politics of the private sphere to escape our attention as we continue to improve women's opportunities in the public sphere. To do so is not only to concede an increasingly intense site of political engagement to the machinations of hegemonic consumer culture, but also to abandon an important opportunity to effect meaningful change in the everyday lives of diverse women.

[1] I refer to the public/private division throughout this paper because it has been, and arguably still is, a useful theoretical device. Nevertheless, the problems associated with translating this theoretical model to real lived experience should not be ignored. While some feminists have used this division to argue against women's exclusion from the public sphere and to render women's private sphere work visible, others have argued that the binary is too rigid to be meaningful. In this article, I am using the division as a broad, shorthand way in which to recognize the hegemonic separation between the private, domestic sphere associated with the feminine world of unpaid work, consumption and reproduction, and the public sphere of paid employment, associated with the masculine world of production. An excellent discussion of the indeterminacy of the public/private divide and the inability of the binary to recognize racial and class-based difference is provided by Susan Boyd (1997).

[2] See Brodie (1995, 1996); Bashevkin (1998).

[3] *Maxim* Magazine, which began publishing in the United States in 1997, boasts newsstand sales of over 800,000 and has inspired copy cat periodicals such as FHM (*For Him Magazine*) and *Gear*. Since the arrival of *Maxim*, staple men's magazines like GQ (*Gentlemen's Quarterly*) and *Details* have included significantly more pictures of scantily clad women than ever before. Despite this, *Maxim* had double the circulation of it's nearest rival in 1999, according to figures from the Audit Bureau of Circulations. The growing acceptability of the magazine is also reflected by the fact that *Maxim* recently dropped its original tag line, "For Men Who Should Know Better," replacing it only with the words, "For Men."

[4] For discussion of the computer industry and women's work see Menzies (1996). Feminist analysis of the language of digital culture is provided by Herring *et al.* (1995).

[5] There is one notable exception to this general trend. See Silverstone and Hirsch (1992).

[6] Interestingly, while there is a growing body of work in the field of "women and technology," there remains relatively little research on the construction of masculinity and technology. Notable exceptions are Pursell (1979, 1993);

Mohun (1996, 1997); Cockburn (1983).

[7]Autumn Stanley provides thorough discussion of women's contributions to the invention of numerous kinds of technology, including domestic technology. See Stanley (1993). Nevertheless, there remains much work to be done in this area, especially in the contemporary context.

[8]Existing literature is dominated by urban studies. For discussion of the rural experience, see Jensen (1986); Jellison (1993); Davis (1993); Rile (1990, 1988).

[9]North American historical literature is dominated by the monographs of Ruth Schwartz Cowan (1983). For a similar discussion of the Canadian context see Strong-Boag (1985).

[10]The first monograph dedicated to exploring the historical relationships between gender, technology and consumption appeared in 1998. See Roger Horowitz and Arwen Mohun, eds., *His and Hers: Gender, Consumption and Technology* (1998). See also, Joy Parr, *Domestic Goods: The Material, the Moral and the Economic in the Postwar Years* (1999).

[11]The major academic monographs that explore domestic technologies and the history of housework in North America are Ruth Schwartz Cowan's *More Work For Mother: The Ironies of Household Technology from the Open Hearth to the Microwave* (1983) and Susan Strasser's *Never Done: A History of American Housework* (1982). Both end their studies in the early 1960s.

[12]It is important to note that the environmental problems associated with using such vast quantities of cleanser are ignored in the name of maintaining a perpetually clean shower.

[13]An analysis of products advertised in two periodicals from the domestic improvement genre in the last five years bears this out. *Popular Mechanics* (a magazine marketed primarily to men), included virtually *no* advertisements for domestic appliances designed for housework or cooking, while *Better Homes and Gardens* (marketed primarily to women), dedicated less than five percent of its advertising space to lawn mowers and power tools.

[14]This analysis, based on the work of Sut Jhally (1987), consisted of coding approximately three hundred commercials obtained from the Television Bureau of Canada, dating from 1970 to the present. The full semiotic and quantitative analysis is included in my forthcoming dissertation.

[15]Long standing home-interior magazines like *Better Homes and Gardens*, *Ideal Homes*, *Homes and Gardens*, and *House and Garden*, have been joined by numerous new publications since the early 1980s. These include *Interiors*, *Country Living*, *Traditional Homes*, *Country Homes and Interiors*, *House Beauti-*

ful, *Elle Decoration*, *Metropolitan Home*, and *Period Living*. See Usherwood (1997).

[16]According to Ernst Dichter, "Marriage today is not only the culmination of a romantic attachment...it is also a decision to create a partnership in establishing a comfortable home, equipped with a great number of products" (qtd. in Friedan 1963). This is arguably even more evident in our hypermodern consumer society.

[17]Canadian communications theorist Marshall McLuhan (1967) was one of the first to recognize the relationship between gendered imagery and new technologies. Ellen Lupton (1993) takes this work further by examining American twentieth century design history from the perspective of female consumers and users. The use of gendered images in technology discourse is also examined in Balsamo (1996); Millar (1998); Springer (1996).

References

Arneil, Barbara. *Politics and Feminism*. Oxford: Blackwell, 1999.

Balsamo, Anne. *Technologies of the Gendered Body: Reading Cyborg Women* Durham, NC: Duke University Press, 1996.

Bashevkin, Sylvia. *Women on the Defensive: Living Through Conservative Times*. Toronto: University of Toronto Press, 1998.

Benston, Margaret Lowe. "Women's Voices/Men's Voices: Technology as Language." *Inventing Women: Science, Technology and Gender*. Eds. G. Kirup and L. S. Keller. Cambridge: Polity, 1992.

Bereano, Philip, Christine Bose and Erik Arnold. "Kitchen Technology and the Liberation of Women from Housework." Eds. Wendy Faulkner and Erik Arnold. *Smothered by Invention: Technology in Women's Lives*. London: Pluto Press, 1985. 162-82.

Bose, Christine. "Technology and Changes in the Division of Labour in the American Home." *Women's Studies International Quarterly* 2 (3) (1979): 295-304.

Boyd, Susan. "Challenging the Public/Private Divide: An Overview." *Challenging the Public/Private Divide: Feminism, Law and Public Policy*. Ed. Susan Boyd. Toronto: University of Toronto Press, 1997. 3-37.

Brodie, Janine. *Politics on the Margins: Restructuring and the Canadian Women's Movement*. Halifax: Fernwood, 1995.

Brodie, Janine. *Women and Canadian Public Policy*. Toronto: Harcourt Brace, 1996.

Melanie Stewart Millar

Busch, Jane. "Cooking Competition: Technology on the Domestic Market in the 1930s." *Technology and Culture* 24 (2) (1983): 222-245.

Cockburn, Cynthia. *Brothers: Male Dominance and Technological Change.* London: Pluto Press, 1983.

Cooper, Steve. "Home Offices: Well Within Your Reach." *Better Homes and Gardens.* (November 1996): 144.

Cowan, Ruth Schwartz. *More Work For Mother: The Ironies of Household Technology from the Open Hearth to the Microwave.* New York: Basic Books, 1983.

Davis, Angela E. "Valiant Servants: Women and Technology on the Canadian Prairies, 1910-1940." *Manitoba History* 25 (1993): 33-42.

Day, Tanis. "Substituting Capital for Labour in the Home: the Diffusion of Household Technology." PhD. Dissertation, Queen's University at Kingston, 1987.

Friedan, Betty. *The Feminine Mystique.* New York: Norton and Co., 1963.

Hare, Melanie and Laura C. Johnson. "Alternatives to Working from Home." WE *International* 46/47 (Winter 1999): 31.

Herring, Susan, Deborah A. Johnson and Tamra Di Benedetto. "This Discussion Has Gone Too Far!: Male Resistance to Female Participation on the Internet." *Gender Articulated: Language and the Socially Constructed Self.* Eds. Kira Hall and Mary Bulcholtz. New York: Routledge, 1995.

Horowitz, Roger and Arwen Mohun, eds. *His and Hers: Gender, Consumption and Technology.* Charlottesville and London: University Press of Virginia, 1998.

Hoy, Suellen. 'The Garbage Dispose, the Public Health and the Good Life," *Technology and Culture* 26 (4) (October 1985): 758-784.

Jackson, Maggie. "Link Between Home and Work Dissolves." *The Toronto Star* November 17, 1999: D6.

Jhally, Sut. *The Codes of Advertising: Fetishism and the Political Economy of Meaning in the Consumer Society.* London: Frances Pinter, 1987.

Jensen, Joan. *Loosening the Bonds: Mid-Atlantic Farm Women, 1750-1850.* New Haven, Conn., 1986.

Jellison, Katherine. *Entitled to Power: Farm Women and Technology, 1913-65.* Chapel Hill, N.C., 1993.

Kapstein, Ethan Barnaby. "The Solar Cooker." *Technology and Culture* 22 (1) (January 1981): 112-121.

Kaufman, Gayle. "The Portrayal of Men's Family Roles on Television Commercials." *Sex Roles* 41 (5,6) (1999): 440-441.

Kemp, Sandra and Judith Squires, eds. *Feminisms*. New York: Oxford University Press, 1997.

Lubar, Steven. "Men/Women/Production/ Consumption." *His and Hers: Gender, Consumption and Technology*. Eds. Roger Horowitz and Arwen Mohun. Charlottesville and London: University Press of Virginia, 1998.

Lupton, Ellen. *Mechanical Brides: Women and Machines from Home to Office*. New York: Princeton Architectural Press, 1993.

Luxton, Meg. *More Than a Labour of Love*. Toronto: Women's Educational Press, 1980.

McLuhan, Marshall. *The Mechanical Bride: The Folklore of Industrial Man*. Boston: Beacon Press, 1967.

Menzies, Heather. *Whose Brave New World?* Toronto: Between the Lines, 1996.

Millar, Melanie Stewart. *Cracking the Gender Code: Who Rules the Wired World?* Toronto: Second Story Press, 1998.

Mohun, Arwen. "Why Mrs. Harrison Never Learned to Iron: Gender, Skill and Mechanization in the Steam Laundry Industry." *Gender and History* 8 (1996): 231-51.

Mohun, Arwen. "Laundrymen Construct Their World: Gender and the Transformation of a Domestic Task into an Industrial Process." *Technology and Culture* 38 (1) (January 1997): 31-40.

Mumford, Steven. "Comfort Kitchens" *Better Homes and Gardens* (November 1996): 119-126.

Oakley, Ann. *The Sociology of Housework*. London: Martin Robertson, 1974.

Ocran, Amanda Araba. "Across the Home/Work Divide: Homework in Garment Manufacture and the Failure of Employment Regulation." Ed. Susan B. Boyd. *Challenging the Public/Private Divide: Feminism, Law and Public Policy*. Toronto: University of Toronto Press, 1997. 144-167.

Parr, Joy. *Domestic Goods: The Material, the Moral and the Economic in the Postwar Years*. Toronto: University of Toronto Press, 1999.

Phizacklea, Annie and Carol Wolkowitz. *Homeworking Women: Gender, Racism and Class at Work* London: Sage, 1995.

Pursell, Carroll. "Toys, Technology and Sex Roles in America, 1920-1940." *Dynamos and Virgins Revisited: Women and Technological Change*. Ed. Martha Moore Trescott. Metchuen, NJ and London: Scarecrow, 1979.

Pursell, Carroll. "The Construction of Masculinity in Technology." *Polhem* 11 (1993): 206-219.

Rakow, Lana. *Gender on the Line*. Urbana and Chicago: University of Illinois

Press, 1992.

Rile, Glenda. "In or Out of the Historical Kitchen? Interpretations of Minnesota Rural Women." *Minnesota History* 52 (1990): 61-71.

Rile, Glenda. *The Female Frontier: A Comparative View of Women on the Prairie and the Plains.* Laurence, Kansas, 1988.

Sardar, Ziauddin and Jerome R. Ravetz, eds. *Cyberfutures: Culture and Politics of the Information Superhighway.* New York: New York University Press, 1996.

Seager, Joni. *The State of Women in the World Atlas.* London: Penguin, 1997.

Segal, Lynne. *Slow Motion: Changing Masculinities, Changing Men.* London: Virago, 1990.

Silverstone, Roger and Eric Hirsch, eds. *Consuming Technologies: Media and Information in Domestic Spaces.* London and New York: Routledge, 1992.

Springer, Claudia. *Electronic Eros: Bodies and Desire in the Postindustrial Age.* Austin: Texas University Press, 1996.

Southex Exhibitions Inc., 2000 National Home Show Media Kit. April 7 – April 16, 2000, Toronto, Ontario.

Stanley, Autumn. *Mothers and Daughter of Invention: Notes for a Revised History of Technology.* New Brunswick, New Jersey: Rutgers, 1993.

Strasser, Susan. *Never Done: A History of American Housework.* New York: Pantheon Books, 1982.

Strong-Boag, Veronica. "Discovering the Home: The Last 150 Years of Domestic Work in Canada." *Women's Paid and Unpaid Work: Historical and Contemporary Perspectives.* Ed. Paula Bourne. Toronto: New Hogtown Press, 1985. 35-61.

Wacjman, Judy. "Domestic Technology: Labour Saving or Enslaving? Eds. Gill Kirkup and Laurie Smith Keller. *Inventing Women: Science, Gender and Technology.* Cambridge: Polity Press, 1992.

Usherwood, Barbara. "Transnational Publishing: The Case of *Elle Decoration.*" *Buy This Book: Studies in Advertising and Consumption.* Eds. Mica Nava, Andrew Blake, Iain MacRury and Barry Richards. London and New York: Routledge, 1997. 178-190.

Communal Kitchens in Peru and Mexico

Lucy Luccisano

Over the past two decades, market-oriented development strategies have transformed the relationship between the state, the economy, and civil society in Latin America. Neo-liberal structural adjustment policies have produced new conceptualizations of social development and poverty alleviation. In response to fiscal deficits and inefficiencies, public expenditures on social services, health, housing, and education, have been drastically curtailed. A significant degree of responsibility for social welfare has been transferred from the federal state to non-governmental agencies and community organizations. These policies have produced profound social dislocation and a dramatic degeneration in standards of living. The responsibility of responding to the day-to-day deprivations brought on by new levels of poverty and economic insecurity have fallen disproportionately on the shoulders of poor women.

One response to women's daily struggles has been the organization of communal kitchens, where women gather with one another to provide meals for their families. Communal kitchens have facilitated the entry of Peruvian and Mexican women into the public sphere and opened up a political space that has challenged gender boundaries and power configurations in personal relationships. These organized collective efforts have drawn attention to the significance of women's organizations for community development in Latin America and to the link between survival strategies of and empowerment for poor women. This paper addresses such issues by exploring women's experiences in community kitchens in Peru and Mexico.[1] Despite different origins—

in Peru the kitchens were a grassroots response to austerity measures implemented in the late '70s, and in Mexico they were part of a government strategy to alleviate poverty in the early 1990s—in both countries they have been used to cushion the hardships caused by economic restructuring.

Theoretical Overview

In her research on women's activism in Latin America, Maxine Molyneux argues that it is important to distinguish mobilization efforts motivated by "practical gender" interests from those motivated by "strategic gender" interests (1985: 230-235). Poor women, she suggests, are more likely to organize around practical gender interests that are rooted in the traditional sexual division of labour and include the everyday needs of food, housing, and economic survival. Strategic gender interests, which transcend women's traditional roles, include the attainment of reproductive rights, the establishment of legal and social measures to ensure gender equality, and the initiatives aimed at passing legislation on violence against women. Molyneux argues that the "formulation of strategic interests can only be effective as a form of intervention when full account is taken of these practical gender interests" (1985:234). This kind of dualistic approach, which is rarely used to conceptualize feminist struggles, is highly problematic when applied to poor women's activism in the "third world." The implication of using this dualistic approach to describe poor women's struggles, as Amy Lind points out, is that poor women in Latin America would appear to not have "a strategic agenda beyond their economic welfare" (1992:137). To develop a comprehensive understanding of the political significance of communal kitchens, it is essential that we conceptualize women's survival strategies and their political learning and engagement as part of the same political process.

A distinct feature of the struggles of poor Latin American women is that they enter the public sphere through gendered familial obligations. As Elizabeth Jelin argues, when women enter the public sphere—even for the purpose of obtaining basic domestic objectives—they begin to view themselves differently. Specifically, their "active presence in the family, a unit of social reproduction but not strictly domestic, opens up new spaces for popular female participation and transforms the initial idea that situates women within the confines of the family" (Jelin 1990:189). This more inclusive conceptualization of poor women's strategies situates their struggles as part of transformative gender politics that challenge the boundaries between the personal and the political, the private and the public, and practical gender interests and strategic gender interests.

Peruvian Communal Kitchens

Communal strategies are not new to Peruvian women who have always depended on self-help measures to deal with the difficulties of everyday life. Indeed, since the late '70s, Peruvian women have worked communally to combat hunger in their neighbourhoods. The first communal kitchens, interestingly enough, drew on the experience of the "common cooking pots," which were organized during the national strikes against the implementation of International Monetary Fund's (IMF) austerity measures in 1977 (Lora 2000). The '80s saw the first occurrence of grassroots communal cooking, and by 1986 it was estimated that there were "700 communal kitchens in Lima, in which 14,000 poor women participated to provide for 70,000 beneficiaries" (Diaz 1986: 8). These women were largely very poor, illiterate, middle-aged migrants who had left poverty and violence in rural areas (Lind and Farmelo 1996). The socio-demographics of these women differed from those participating in the kitchens after 1990, where most women were younger, institutionally educated, and held professional occupations, such as teachers and nurses. Sometimes these women were the children of the rural migrants.

The efforts of communal kitchens were supported by various philanthropic agencies and, in particular, by religious-based agencies including CARITAS (the International Aid Organization of the Catholic Church), OFASA (Adventist), and SEPAS (Evangelical), and CARE (secular). Indeed, in 1979, an agreement between the United States Agency for International Development (USAID) and the Peruvian government allowed for surplus agricultural products to be donated to Peru and made available to communal kitchens through philanthropic agencies and the state. During the '80s and the early '90s, CARITAS also played a central and leading role in providing food supplies to the kitchens. In the 1980s, the community kitchens also facilitated the formation of Christian-based communities, popularizing the theology of liberation otherwise known as the "church of the poor" (Blondet 1995: 262). This theology, which privileges the concerns of the economically disenfranchised, advocates collective struggles for social reform and economic justice and the politicization of poverty and hunger.

The state also subsidized various types of women's organizations. Fernando

Belaúnde's National Action Party (*Acción Popular*, AP) (1980-1985) provided kitchen infrastructure and donated food for the operation of "Family Kitchens" to women who supported his governing party (Barrig 1996: 60). Alan Gracia's American Popular Revolutionary Alliance (*Alianza Popular Revolucionaria de América*, APRA) government (1985-1990) implemented a number of programs to deal with the poor, including the Direct Assistance Program (*Programa de Asistencia Directa*, PAD). Through PAD, the government provided subsidies for community organizations including community kitchens; however, it developed a clientalistic approach to the community kitchens and controlled the developments within them, in fact, using these kitchens as a way of gaining voter support for the 1990 presidential elections (Barrig 1996: 62). While some community kitchens welcomed state subsidies, many choose to remain relatively autonomous from state assistance and political manipulation and were able to do so because they were being subsidized by other non-governmental organizations such as CARITAS. In fact, during this period, 500 kitchens in Lima were under the auspices of CARITAS (Barrig 1996:62).

After winning the 1990 presidential elections in Peru, Alberto Fujimori's Change 90-New Majority (*Cambio 90-Nueva Mayoría*, C90-NM) government (1990-1995) implemented a severe stabilization program to combat a prolonged recession and to reintegrate Peru into the international financial market. Market-based re-structuring meant deregulation of the financial and labour markets, privatization of public enterprises, a broadening of the tax base system, and a reduction in tax evasion. Included in these changes were drastic reductions in price subsidies, social spending, and public sector employment, and increased interest rates and taxes on government services (Roberts 1996: 96). These structural adjustments were initially implemented without any poverty relief programs to mitigate the economic consequences for low-income and poor people. Although the National Compensation and Development Fund (*Fondo Nacional de Compensación y Desarrollo Social*, FONCODES), a social co-investment fund program providing infrastructure and poverty relief, was established in 1991, it was improperly managed. In 1992 it had spent less than 20 percent of its budget. In 1994 $170 million was budgeted for FONCODES but only $45 million was spent during the first six months (Roberts, 1996:103 nt64). Thus, during Fujimori's first term in office, 54% of Peruvians were living in poverty.

In the absence of a federal emergency social-safety net, poor and low-income women—including teachers, nurses and public employees—turned to communal kitchens and other self-help strategies. The kitchens proliferated throughout Peru and by the early 1990s, 40,000 low-income women gathered at 2,000 sites to feed 200,000 persons in Lima alone (Lind and Farmelo 1996). Because of the cost of food, many women living in the same neighbourhoods pooled their resources to purchase and prepare food communally to minimize cost. In the kitchens, responsibilities were shared, and duties, including accounting practices, food purchases, food preparation, and cleaning were organized on a rotating basis. To cover their costs, the women charged a small fee for each meal. Various philanthropic organizations donated food to the kitchens and this support, though minimal, provided much needed assistance.

The benefits of participating in communal kitchens went beyond the provision of food. The kitchens were centres of personal growth and political awareness[2] which have had unforeseen political effects. The kitchens allowed women to enter public spaces and to engage in community action. They gained a better understanding of themselves, their capacities, and the world around them. The wide-ranging benefits of involvement in the kitchens were a constant theme in the interviews I conducted. As Rosa—a mother of four— commented, "I really like being involved in the organizing aspect of the communal kitchens. I enjoy the responsibility and the interactions I have with the other women" (Interview: Lima, August 1991). Gina, a mother of three, said "I'm so busy these days I run from one meeting to another, I have no time for myself, but I love the activity in my life, I love the friendships. I can't stay at home anymore I get so bored" (Interview: Lima, August 1991). It was also within these spaces that women challenged one another to resolve their conflicts, to take on greater responsibilities within their communities, and to assume positions of leadership both within their organizations and in other grassroots organizations.

The interviews I conducted also suggest that collective work in the kitchens initiated a process during which women broke their silence and began to voice their ideas, concerns, and anger. Through their daily discussions and participation in workshops, these women acquired the cultural-discursive resources that facilitated the exchange of knowledge mediated in language (Schild 1991: 13). In a neighbourhood meeting attended by 150 kitchen members, a number of women spoke of their experiences of empowerment. Women talked about how they had learned that they have rights, including the right to speak, to be heard, and to be respected. Vicky, a participant, articulated this theme: "I am a poor woman, but I have rights. I have a right to live a life of dignity and of freedom. I have a right to be respected and not to be mistreated or abused by my husband or others" (Participant-observation of a community meeting: Lima, July 1991). Indeed, a discourse about rights was expressed in most of the women's testimonies.

Chantal Mouffe's concept of "contradictory interpellation" is helpful in understanding the political importance of rights discourse. "Contradictory interpellation" is manifested in the contradiction between the principle that as citizens women are equal to men, but in their everyday experiences they are treated as secondary to men (Mouffe 1988:95). Mouffe argues "subjects constructed in subordination by a set of discourses are, at the same time, interpellated as equal by other discourses" (1988:95). According to this view, Peruvian women by engaging in a rights discourse are actively challenging the sexist discourses of *machismo* and are engaged in constituting new subject positions.

This "politicization of the personal" impacted on their relationships. They began to challenge power relations in their everyday lives, with their husbands, women, religious authority figures, and non-governmental organization (NGO) professionals in their communities. Maria, a leader in her kitchen and a community activist, for example, spoke of the enormous changes she had observed in the women in her kitchen:

> At first the women would come to the kitchen and follow the instruction of the more experienced women like myself. After a few months of being together, the women no longer avoided my eyes when they talked to me but looked directly at me and at the persons they were addressing. They also challenged one another as well as many of my ideas. Even I had to get used to a more confident group of women. (Interview: Lima, August 1991)

As women gained the confidence to challenge the power relations in their lives, conflict over decision-making in the kitchens arose. While some of the conflicts could be resolved, other conflicts resulted in some women leaving the kitchens to participate in other kitchens. As Maria stated, "women will no longer put up with dictators and this is a positive sign. We welcome the freedom to voice difference in the kitchens and we need to learn to deal with difference" (Interview: Lima, August 1991). Conflict and negotiation were not seen as negative but were understood as an integral part of political learning and growth.

These women have also learned to publicly voice their demands to the state, and consequently, communal kitchens have developed into a strategic social movement in Peru. For example, the autonomous kitchens belonging to the Federation of Self-Managed Popular Kitchens (*Federación de Comedores Populares Autogestionarios*, FCPA) made several demands on the state and achieved a new legal status for their kitchens as a "social base group" in 1988 (Lind, 1996). Lind notes that as a popular women's movement, "their perspectives and demands have elicited a great deal of attention from NGOs, political parties, feminist activists, church groups and other base groups who work in poor neighbourhoods" (1996). They have developed into an important and strategic social movement and their demands cannot be ignored by the state.

Until 1993, the communal kitchens were not only spaces of survival and activism, but were also dangerous political spaces. The Shining Path (*Sendero Luminoso*), a violent Maoist guerrilla movement, considered grassroots organizations to be the handmaiden of capitalism. In particular, *Sendero* targeted the communal kitchens, which were seen as a barrier to the much-awaited revolution. Many communal kitchens and grassroots organizations received threats, others were infiltrated, and some became victims of the Shining Path's violence. Between 1991 and early 1992, 40 grassroots leaders were murdered, 10 of whom were women (Barrig 1998: 118). One of the chilling examples of this violence took place on February 15, 1992 when María Elena Moyano, a feminist, community activist and the deputy mayor of *Villa El Salvador*, was shot in the head in front of her two children and then blown up with 11 pounds of dynamite at a fund-raising event. The day before her murder, Moyano had announced at a public rally that "we are not with those who kill popular leaders, who massacre leaders of soup kitchens and Glass of Milk programs" (Galvin 1992: A10). Because of her courageous commitment to feminist politics, Moyano now serves as the symbol for a re-presentation of poor Latin America women. The murder of Moyano did not enfeeble poor women's struggles for survival; with mixed emotions of fear, anger, and love, they continue to provide for their families.

Since the mid-1990s, the politicized space created by communal kitchens was increasingly co-opted and re-deployed by Fujimori's government to promote neo-liberal welfare measures and clientalistic practices. When, for example, privatization of the telephone and telecommunications industries in 1994 proved lucrative, Fujimori directed a substantial sum of monies to social programs, including the national food assistance program (*Programa Nacional de Asistencia Alimentario*, PRONAA) (Roberts 1996:104). Through this program, the state assumed a more important role in the administration of food-aid to communal kitchens. As Nora, a community activist, comments, "the help of the government is minimal but the control is maximum" (Interview: Toronto, April 2000). The actual food support the government provided to communal kitchens was very little and most kitchens could manage without this support. However, this food support program served to strengthen Fujimori's populist practices.

For example, during the 2000 presidential election campaign, Fujimori drew heavily on electoral re-election populist strategies. Given that more than 42 percent of Peruvian households currently receive food-subsidies, communal kitchens had become indispensable sources of political manipulation and support.[3] Fujimori cut off aid to 150 of 2,203 kitchens in Lima that had refused to support his political campaign. Although PRONAA argued that health standards, rather than political interests, were the motivation, Relinda Sosa Pérez, president of the Federation of Community Kitchens of Lima and Collao (FECCPALC), maintained that this was clearly a political act (Garcia 2000). PRONAA, she argued, forced the women to hang Fujimori's political propaganda in the kitchens, to attend public political rallies, and to endorse his campaign through the signing of petitions (Garcia 2000). According to Sosa Pérez, if the women chose not to participate, then "there's no food ... (t)hat's what PRONAA officials have told us in the supply centers in Lima where we go to pick up food. Many groups have given in because hunger doesn't wait. If they don't say anything, it's because they can't prove that the threat was made." (Garcia 2000). The government has not only appropriated and institutionalized survival strategies, it has also engaged in a "divide and rule" strategy to disrupt women's organizations, de-politicize the relationship between gender and food, and individualize poverty.

A daily popular television talk show, hosted by Laura Bozzo, was a useful technique to solidify the link between food-aid and Fujimori's government in people's minds. Throughout her show, Bozzo offered prizes and gifts to women who participated in the kitchens, invited women from the kitchens to appear on the show, and provided overall support for the government (Interview: Toronto, April 2000). Fujimori also co-opted community female leaders into the ranks of his party and other pro-government groups such as "Let's Go Neighbour" (*Vamos Vecino*) to attract women voters (Garcia 2000).

The above-mentioned strategies outline some of the new configurations of power relations in Peru. Although it is too early to predict the political responses of Peruvian women, it is clear that they recognize their triumphs, are continuing in their struggles, and have not given up hope for a better life for themselves and their children. Luz-Maria, a community leader, argues that:

In 10 years we have gained more voices that speak in favour of women. We find hope, struggle, and creativity in women's spaces and we learn how to work as a team, and while unions and other institutions have crumpled in the last ten years the communal kitchens have resisted, through the strength of women as mothers, we have survived. (Interview: Toronto, April 2000)

Through their public and collective participation of traditional gendered responsibilities, these women have given a new meaning to political activism. Indeed, their daily survival struggles, which are no longer seen as apolitical private domestic responsibilities, challenge the boundary between the private sphere and the public sphere and between practical gender interests and strategic gender interests.

Mexican Community Kitchens

In contrast to the Peruvian example, community kitchens in Mexico began as an institutionalized welfare practice. Introduced as part of President Carlos Salinas' (1988-1994) market-based economic reform program, the National Solidarity Program (PRONASOL), an umbrella program provided infrastructure, education, health, food assistance, and income-generating programs to the poor through many government agencies. In particular, PRONASOL funds were made available to the government agency Integrated Family Development (*Desarrolo Integral de la Familia*, DIF), for a nutritional assistance program called Popular Kitchens and Integrated Services Units (*Cocinas Populares y Unidades de Servicios Integrales*, COPUSI). This was not the first instance of community kitchens, as the Women's Regional Council of the National Council of the Urban Popular Movement (CONAMUP) did operate a few independent community kitchens in Mexico City. Because of the experience of those few kitchens, the Women's Regional Council pressured the Ministry of Social Development to fund these types of programs (Stephen 1997: 152). In part due to local pressures and to international support for these types of programs,[4] the Salinas government implemented the program of community kitchens. In most states, the COPUSI[5] program arranged for the kitchens to purchase the necessary infrastructure, such as ovens and refrigerators, provided basic groceries, and used community labour in the management of the kitchens. The program was offered to organized communities of 40 families or more.

Like the Peruvian examples, these kitchens were administered by a team of women responsible for accounting, purchasing food, cooking, and cleaning. By 1998, there were 5,082 community kitchens operating in urban areas in Mexico. The kitchens provided breakfasts for children under the age of six, pregnant and lactating women, the elderly, and the disabled in poor neighbourhoods. Meals were sold at a subsidized cost and the profits were re-invested to cover the cost of the program. In some communities, workshops on health and nutrition and other activities developed alongside the community kitchens. Women who volunteered in the kitchens participated with neighbourhood women in the workshops, which included a range of classes from skills training, to sewing and artwork, and self-improvement activities such as exercise programs and beauty courses.

The community kitchens program was expanded under Ernesto Zedillo's government (1994-2000). Zedillo had inherited an economy in crisis. Throughout the last year of Salinas' administration, unexpected shocks, including the Chiapas uprising and political assassinations, resulted in the capital flight of billions of dollars. The Mexican government hoped for a regeneration of its reserves through foreign investment funds. However, this did not occur and existing investors panicked and pulled their investments out of Mexico in December of 1994 (DeLong 1997). In response, the value of the peso fell by more than sixty-percent (DeLong 1997). Zedillo's administration, in early 1995, was forced to negotiate a rescue package with the United States and the International Monetary Fund, which included borrowing $40 billion (DeLong 1997). In Mexico, a stabilization reform package was implemented based on austerity measures, increased privatization, and a wage freeze. In response to these measures, Zedillo continued several existing programs, including the COPUSI kitchen program, and created new programs, such as adding a hot breakfast program to the DIF food program in rural areas.

Based on the communal kitchen format the government provided a monthly food basket to an organized community that then assumed the responsibility for providing breakfasts to mostly school-aged children in rural areas. This program also provided workshops that taught women about nutrition and the preparation of different nutritional foods. For example, the DIF encouraged recipients to cultivate gardens, poultry farms, and fish reservoirs and to use the produce to complement the hot breakfasts. The women also acquired preventive health and medical knowledge in the workshops. In urban areas, where COPUSI community kitchens were absent, groups of organized mothers provided cold breakfasts to children at schools. As of March 1999, there were approximately 400,000 women participating in cold and hot breakfast programs.

Like Peru, community kitchens opened up spaces that produced unforeseen consequences. The interviews suggest that many women in Mexico City were pleased to have a space to gather with other women. Emma, a mother of three, said, "it gives me great pleasure to come to the kitchens" (Interview: Mexico City, June 1995). Lupita, a mother of four and a participant, said, "before my days were spent only with the children, many times I felt alone and depressed, now that I spend time with other women I find that I'm less depressed and happier" (Interview: Mexico City, July 1995). Women also commented that family members and in particular their husbands have noticed changes in them. Another woman, Anna said "my husband says that I've changed since I've participated in these kitchens, and perhaps I have, I now have a different understanding of what it means to be a woman, a wife and a mother" (Interview: Mexico City, July 1995).

However, in both countries, the kitchen responsibilities added more work to their daily domestic duties. The women spoke about the demands of working in the kitchens, which also seemed to add more work to their already over-burdened schedules, doubling or tripling their domestic responsibilities. As Lupita indicated, "when it's my turn to work in the kitchens, my day begins at 5:00 in the morning and ends by midnight. We women are still responsible for taking care of our own children, husbands, and housework" (Interview: Mexico City, July 1995). These activities have not served to challenge women's traditional domestic responsibilities, but rather have reinforced them. The present challenge facing these women is how to negotiate, challenge, and transform the gendered division of labour that has been deepened by policies of neo-liberal economic restructuring.

Although a social movement around community kitchens in particular has yet to develop in Mexico, there exists a more general movement organized around the politics of food and there are numerous examples of self-help activism. In response to the 1990 changes in the government tortilla subsidy, for example, the Women's Regional Council (*Regional de Mujeres*) and the Pact Against Hunger (*Pacto Contra Hambre*) movement took to the streets with pots and pans to protest. By 1995, the Women's Regional Council, involved in some 20 communal kitchens that received the COPUSI program in Mexico City, began to offer workshops on law in addition to other self-help workshops. For these women, kitchens offered sites for political learning and mobilization. Pilar, a participant and community leader, pointed out that one important conflict experienced with the DIF was its refusal to understand that the kitchens were organizations. She states, "we can't get them to understand that this is an organization, a place where cooking is among one of the many activities that take place in our organization" (Interview: Mexico City, August 1995). Significantly, these more politicized kitchens have developed good working relationships with the DIF. The Women's Regional Council felt they could engage in serious conversations with the DIF that would allow them to define their needs, and many times this entailed challenging the DIF's interpretation of needs. During the peso crisis, for example, the women negotiated a more favourable schedule for their kitchen infrastructure loans. While the kitchens generally operate on a voluntary basis, one kitchen has started to financially compensate its women and the Women's Regional Council has entered into discussions with the DIF about extending this practice to other kitchens.

Concluding Thoughts

As these cases demonstrate, through participation in communal kitchens, women have begun to challenge the common-sense meanings and identities that construct women's traditional roles in Latin America. Pilar, a community activist in Mexico, stated that "the children of these women will grow up with a different understanding of the meaning of women as mothers, as they will have observed the struggles and activism of their mothers" (Interview: Mexico City, August 1995). The experience of empowerment is understood as being linked to an on-going process of struggle. As Luz-Maria, a Peruvian activist, so poignantly argues:

> We must continue to struggle, our work continues to bring about a linking of the chains of solidarity. We don't see the kitchen as a place of reducing women to their domestic duties, but as places where women have responded with their hearts to difficult economic situations. When women gather, we find spaces of hope, of struggle, of creativity, a space of sharing sentiments, of course we fight, we struggle but when we come together we learn how to work as a team. I have hope but it's hard, changes are slow, we may get tired, but we have hope, we fight daily, as fighting is a part of life, we also have a capacity to celebrate, to be joyful and this helps us woman to woman. (Interview: Toronto, April 2000)

In embracing a more overtly political agenda, many of the kitchens are also becoming an important part of the broader "popular" and urban women's movements that are struggling to redefine women's rights and the meaning of social citizenship. Luz-Maria, for example, spoke of the global chains of solidarity and how her organization is networking with women in other countries. This "international solidarity," she mused, "does not make us feel alone in our struggles, it gives us more hope and strength" (Interview: Toronto, April 2000). Although most of the women expressed exhaustion and frustration, they are committed to continuing their struggle. "We are fighting," Pilar explained, "not for survival strategies, but for a strategy of life" (Interview: August, Mexico City 1995). It is armed with this commitment to collective struggle that the women of Peru and Mexico enter the new millennium.

Despite these successes, it is important to recognize that these women are facing contradictions that threaten to undermine their new-found power. Their ability to keep their families alive during periods of brutal economic hardship has not gone unnoticed by the state. Since the mid-1990s community kitchens in Peru—which have been a form of survival for more than 20 years— have become an inexpensive welfare and electoral strategy for the state. Indeed, on a global level, government agendas and policies are based on replacing institutionalized welfare practices with volunteerism on the part of citizens. Consequently, the feminization of poverty is becoming more firmly entrenched as uncontested notions of gendered activities are incorporated into state welfare strategies. The challenge that lies ahead for feminist struggles will be to strengthen global networks of solidarity and develop strategies to subvert and contest the increasing incorporation of gender-based volunteerism. It is this challenge which is on the edge of feminist struggles for the new millennium.

I wish to thank Peruvian and Mexican women who gave of their time to speak me about their lives, their struggles, and their triumphs. I wish to thank Lorna Erwin, Paula Maurutto, Alan Simmons, Ruth Urbach, and Mariana Valverde who read and made valuable comments throughout various drafts and Alejandra Ortiz who helped with Spanish translation. I also wish to thank the editors of this volume and the anonymous reader who provided many useful suggestions. Any errors or shortcomings in the analysis are the sole responsibility of the author.

[1]This article is based on research conducted in the early and mid-1990s, in

Lima, Peru, and Mexico City, Mexico, on anti-poverty programs. It draws on semi-structured interviews and participant observation. Recent interviews with Peruvian women in Toronto also inform the discussion. To protect confidentiality pseudonyms are used.

[2]The communal kitchens are not uniform. The nature of the organization of the kitchen informs the type of experience the women gain. Even though they receive food aid from donors, many of these kitchens are relatively autonomous organisations. Some kitchens are the result of social welfare programs.

[3]The USAID program in Peru, the second-largest in Latin America and U.S. bilateral aid, including food aid and disaster relief and rehabilitation, totalled more than $1.2 billion during the 1990-99 period. (U.S. Department of State, March 2000 Bureau of Western Hemisphere Affairs) http://www.state.gov/www/background_notes/peru_0300_bgn.html#relations

[4]The United Nations Children's Fund (UNICEF) provided funds to purchase kitchen equipment and medical equipment. The medical equipment was used to measure the nutritional impact of the COPUSI program on children's health. UNICEF was also instrumental in the design of COPUSI manuals, the development of financial and nutritional programs, and in the state-level evaluation workshops (DIF-UNICEF, 1996: 15).

[5]The following are the names of the kitchens in different states: in Campeche, *Cocinas Escolares* (COESCO), (School Kitchens); in Chiapas, *Nutrición y Educación en Solidaridad* (NES) *y Casas Populares para la Alimentación del Niño Desnutrido* (CAPAND), (Nutrition and Education in Solidarity and Popular houses for food for the malnourished child); in Chihuahua and Durango, *Cocinas Rústicas*, (Rustic Kitchens); in Guerrero, *Cocinas Rurales*, (Rural Kitchens); in Oaxaca, *Aula Abierta*, (Open Classroom); in Tabasco, *Programa de Nutrición* (PRONUTRA), (Program of Nutrition); in Tamaulipas, *Desayunos Escolares* (School Breakfasts); and in Veracurz, *Cocinas Communitarias* (Community Kitchens).

References

Barrig, Maruja. "Women, Collective Kitchens, and the Crisis of the State in Peru." *Emergences: Women's Struggles for Livelihood in Latin America*. Eds. John Friedmann, Rebecca Abers, and Lilian Autler. Los Angeles: UCLA Latin American Center Publications, University of California, 1996.

Barrig, Maruja. "Female Leadership, Violence, and Citizenship in Peru." *Women and Democracy*. Eds. Jane Jaquette and Sharon L. Wolchik. Baltimore: The Johns Hopkins University Press, 1998.

Blondet, Cecilia. "In No-Man's Land: Poor Women's Organizations and Political Violence in Lima's Neighborhoods." *Emergences: Women's Struggles for Livelihood in Latin America*. Eds. John Friedmann, Rebecca Abers, and Lilian Autler. Los Angeles: UCLA Latin American Center Publications, University of California, 1996.

Blondet, Cecilia. "Out of the Kitchens and onto the Streets: Women's Activism in Peru." *The Challenge of Local Feminisms*. Ed. Amrita Basu. Boulder, Colorado. Westview Press, Inc., 1995.

DeLong, J. Bradford. "Managing International Financial Disorder: Lessons [?] From the Peso Crisis." http://econ161.berkeley.edu/Comments/managing.html , 1997.

Diaz, J. Albertini. "La alimentacion popular urbana y las estrategias de supervivencia." Unpublished paper. Lima: DESCO, 1986.

Galvin, Kevin. "Peruvian woman paid with her life for defying Shining Path rebels." *The Gazette*, Montreal Wednesday February, 19. 1992: A10.

Garcia, Jorge Manuel. "Winning the Woman's Vote." *Latinamerica Press* 32 (11) (March 27, 2000): 3.

Jelin, Elizabeth, ed. *Women and Social Change in Latin America*. London: Zed Books Limited, 1990.

Kenneth, Roberts. "Neoliberalism and the Transformation of Populism in Latin America: The Peruvian Case" *World Politics* 48 (1) (1996): 82-116.

Lind, Amy Conger. "Power, Gender, and Development: Popular Women's Organizations and the Politics of Needs in Ecuador." *The Making of Social Movements in Latin America: Identity, Strategy, and Democracy*. Eds. Arturo Escobar and Sonia E. Alvarez. Boulder: Westview Press, 1992.

Lind, Amy and Martha Farmelo. "Gender and Urban Social Movements: Women's Community Responses to Restructuring and Urban Poverty." Discussion Paper No. 76, http://www.unrisd.org/engindex/publ/list/dp/dp76/lgovshar.htm, June 1996

Luccisano, Lucy. "Discursos Neoliberales y la Reestructuración de los Programas en contra de la Pobreza: Los Casos de Canadá y México," *Justicia Social y Pobreza* . Campeche: Universidad Autónoma de Campeche, Facultad de Humanidades, 1999.

Lora, Carmen. "Solidarity Perspectives." Peru Solidarity Forum. http://cpi.alter.org.pe/psf/ingles/boletines/boletin28/boletin28.html#NEW SCENES, February 2000.

Molyneux, Maxine. "Mobilization Without Emancipation? Women's Interests, the State, and Revolution in Nicaragua." *Feminist Studies* 11 (21)

Lucy Luccisano

(1985): 227-254.

Mouffe, Chantal. "Hegemony and New Political Subjects:Toward a New Concept of Democracy." *Marxism and the Interpretation of Culture.* Eds. Carl Nelson and Lawrence Grossberg. Chicago: University of Illinois Press, 1988.

Schild, Veronica. "Recasting 'Popular' Movements: Gender and Political Learning the Neighbourhood Organizations in Chile." Paper presented at the CEDLA/CERLACJoint Workshop in Amsterdam, 1991.

Stephen, Lynn. *Women and Social Movements in Latin America.*Austin: University of Texas Press, 1997.

Mexican Government Documents

Acuerdo Para El Programa de Alimentacion y Nutricion Familiar Palabras Del C. Presidente de la Republica Dr. Ernesto Zedillo, Los Pinos, Febrero 1995.

Cocinas Populares y Unidades de Servicios Integrales—Una alternativa para el desarrollo comunitario 1989-1995, Julio de 1996.

DIF, COPUSI, Febrero 1994; DIF, Manual de COPUSI, nd.

DIF, Hacia un Modelo de Seguimiento y Evaluación del Programa de Desayunos Escolares, 15-16 de agosto de 1995.

DIF, El Programa de Cocinas populares Origen y Situación Actual, Documento de Trabajo, Enero de 1998.

DIF, Programas Integral de Desayunos Escolares, no date.

Interviews

Interviews conducted in El Pacifico in the district of San Martin de Porras, in Lima Peru from July to August 1991.

Interviews conducted in Toronto, April 2000 with Peruvian activists during a Toronto visit.

Interviews conducted in Mexico City, Mexico from June to September 1995.

Understanding Strategic Dilemmas and Contested Paradoxes

The Case of Registered Nurses' Organizations and Health System Restructuring

Christine Saulnier

After 20 years or more of economic restructuring, the end of the twentieth century has left feminists wondering what their best strategies are for further advancing social justice issues in the new millennium. Looking back on the era of restructuring in Canada, feminists discern very little in the way of consistency in government actions. On the one hand, neoliberal restructuring, thus far, has undoubtedly affected women in a disproportionately negative way. Women, who were not white, able-bodied, upper or middle class, were much less likely to benefit from a downsized state aimed at increasing economic competitiveness through "free market" policies (Brodie 1995; Bakker 1996). On the other hand, according to Janine Brodie (1995: 15), restructuring "refers to a prolonged and conflict-ridden political process during which old assumptions and shared understandings are challenged and are eventually either rejected or transformed while social forces struggle to achieve a new consensus." Therefore, the very nature of the restructuring process ushered in the possibility of progressive, egalitarian change. Restructuring could address the classist, racist, and paternalistic nature of many postwar Keynesian health and welfare policies and programmes (Brodie 1995).

As feminists consider their positioning in the governance[1] process at the edge of the millennium, we have been left wondering how to resist a process that is threatening our hard fought gains,[2] while not appearing nostalgic for pre-restructuring. If we only *resist* restructuring without proposing ways to advance changes, we may miss opportunities for progressive, transformative change that may occur in the struggle to *influence* it. The question becomes: when approaching restructuring is it better to try to influence its positive (progressive) potential or to resist the restructuring process because of its overwhelmingly negative effects?

The focus of this article is the positioning and strategies of registered nursing organizations and their attempts to resist and influence the McKenna government's restructuring process in the province of New Brunswick from 1987 to 1997. I focus on health system reform in New Brunswick in order to understand how and why different positions were staked out there.

New Brunswick is an important case study. The McKenna government had been championed in the popular media as a "social laboratory" for its innovative social programs and economic initiatives (DeMont 1994). However, the national literature on health reform paid scant attention to its restructuring initiatives, focussing on Ontario and Alberta. With more limited resources and less room to manoeuvre economically, New Brunswick might have been more willing to consider proposals for a broader spectrum of changes than it might previously have considered. Pat and Hugh Armstrong (1996: 199) have argued in their research on health reform in Canada that "[c]oncern over rising expenditures and pressure from various groups working in or using the system have led governments over the years to seek ways of altering decision- making and power relations." Such concerns and pressures may have heightened the possibility for dramatic change in New Brunswick as in other "have-not" provinces. Therefore, New Brunswick is an interesting case study because, while its government may have been willing to consider implementing innovative (even progressive) programs if they were cost-effective, these concerns and pressures may have also heightened the potential for it to implement drastic regressive cutbacks.

In their efforts to intervene in the restructuring process in New Brunswick, I will show that registered nursing organizations took a contradictory stand in relation to registered nurses' role in the delivery of health care. In an attempt to present themselves as professionalized in a neoliberal restructuring climate, the nursing organizations developed proposals for health reform in which nurses could offer quality and cost-effective care. They also used their proposals to attempt to solidify and even expand the distinct boundaries of nursing, while emphasizing their shared competence with the medical profession—the dominant gatekeeper in the health care system. Maybe because they had less to lose and more to gain than physicians, organized nursing has been notable for proposing substantial organizational reform, and for making claims of cost-efficiency (Touhy 1986: 412). However, the reception, impact, and outcome of their proposals have been affected by registered nurses' positioning in the health system.

Registered nurses have been paradoxically positioned in the health system as professional caregivers who are subordinate to physicians, but more privileged than other workers such as registered nursing assistants and orderlies. However, in a time of restructuring, some services that are time-consuming such as psycho-social caring are under attack because they are not easily measured, and thus rationalized, for cost-efficiency. Such services are considered "luxuries' in this system because they do not fit into the assembly-line intensification of the work process.[3] According to McPherson (1996) nurses are being both professionalized and proletarianized. Because of this paradoxical position, their competence as skilled professionals and their policy proposals may go unacknowledged while health system restructuring takes advantage of nurses' "natural" talents and exploits their work as undervalued "women's work." Nursing work is vulnerable to cuts because of its gendered nature (Keddy *et al.*, 1998). As New Brunswick nurse historian Hoyt-Magee (1994: 9) stated, since nurses are "predominantly women, their history binds them together through inequities, [and] devalued work experiences that went unrecognized and marginalized in most aspects of the Province's power structures." However, according to Lucille Auffrey (1994: 17), the then president of NANB argued that "the opportunity for nurses to play a much more significant role in the health care system ha[d] never been greater" than during restructuring. Would these organizations have left nurses better off if they had only tried to *resist* the negative incursions into their practice? Did their attempts to *influence* the process by proposing substantial reforms only open opportunities for nurses to be exploited further?

Theoretical and Conceptual Frameworks

An analysis of the proposals of both the Nurses Association of New Brunswick (NANB) and the New Brunswick Nurses Union (NBNU) provides a clearer understanding of the complex, contradictory nature of neoliberal health system restructuring. To analyze the submissions and briefs they made to the government, I use two theoretical and conceptual frameworks to demonstrate the strategic dilemmas faced by these organizations.

First, I consider whether their proposals would respond to their complex practical and strategic gender needs.[4] Practical gender needs can be addressed by fulfilling daily needs such as providing wages, nutrition, and housing. In contrast, "needs formulated from the socially structured subordinate position of women to men in society" are strategic gender needs (Moser *et al.* 1999: 18). To meet strategic gender needs, policies must improve women's status and promote equity to remove systematic biases and change women's unequal position in society. Initiatives to address such needs would include funding for advocacy groups and legislative provisions for equality such as pay equity and employment equity.

This conceptual framework attributes a certain higher value to meeting women's strategic gender needs because meeting only practical gender needs (while not unimportant because they sometimes diminish women's subordination to men) often perpetuates unequal gender relations. To fulfill strategic gender needs and thus work to transform unequal gender relations would require, according to the second conceptual framework, a critical-thinking approach as opposed to a problem-solving one (Parsons 1995; Gill 1993). A critical-thinking approach would consider how to respond to such needs through strategies aimed at democratic empowerment and systemic change. Using a critical-thinking approach, the questions that should become front and centre in these strategies are those about process and participation and thus knowledge and power. In contrast, a problem-solving approach is about the pragmatic needs of policy makers for systems management.

Using both these conceptual frameworks, I consider what they can reveal about nurses' strategic dilemmas. In doing so, I consider whether it is useful to understand their strategic dilemmas as a choice between a problem-solving approach and a critical-thinking one; and between resisting the proletarianization and other negative effects of restructuring, and influencing the health system restructuring so that both their practical and strategic gender needs would be met. Finally, I consider whether their strategic dilemmas (and those of similarly positioned groups) would be better captured by a more nuanced understanding of the creative tensions between such dualistic conceptualizations.

Organized Nursing: Identifying Health System Problems and Solutions

Before considering nurses' proposals and strategic dilemmas, it is important to understand the impact restructuring has had on nurses' work conditions. The impact of restructuring thus far is such that many nurses have either lost their jobs or been left overworked and underpaid. Newly graduated nurses have not been able to find full time work because the number of casual and part-time positions has increased dramatically. All nurses had little mobility and faced a lot of stress, all of which threatened the supply of nurses available to meet the demand (see Appendix A for more details).

The health care system, according to both nursing organizations, was too focussed on curing illness. Its main problems because of this focus were that the roles of physicians and hospitals were being overestimated, nurses' skills and knowledge underutilized, and adequate resources were not provided for health promotion and other community-based programs (NANB 1991; NBNU 1994). Their solution was to restructure the health care system according to the principles of primary health care[5] (PHC). Depending on the setting,[6] according to NANB and NBNU, the PHC vision of health care delivery should allow nurses to assume an expanded role as primary care givers. The PHC model could also provide ways for nurses with expertise in public health, mental health, and occupational health to contribute to the development and implementation of health promotion and disease prevention policies and strategies (NANB 1991: 2). To best implement PHC, two proposals were advocated: the professional association (NANB) proposed a Bachelor of Nursing as sole entry to practice and both organizations proposed using a shared-competence model to assess the most appropriate health professional as primary care giver. To best understand their decisions to make these proposals, both are examined in more detail.

Improving Educational Standards: A Strategic Goal?

According to NANB, to best assume the role of primary care givers and thus ensure that PHC is effective, nursing must move to a Bachelor of Nursing (BN) as sole entry to practice.[7] The idea, as it was proposed by the Canadian Nurses' Association, was that all BN-prepared nurses would be prepared to take on an expanded role within a system oriented by PHC (Grove 1991: 190). However, even if there is little movement toward PHC, a BN as sole entry to practice was argued to be important for several reasons.[8] Primarily, a BN is one way to define nursing boundaries and thus increase nurses' professional status. Advocating the need for a BN as sole entry to practice was undoubtedly important, as nurses were at a disadvantage as a group (vis à vis physicians), as reflected in their salaries, in their inability to set priorities at the clinical level, and in their educational standards. However, there was some disagreement[9] among nurses and between their organizations about the decision to concentrate resources on improving their educational standards.

The heart of the disagreement between the two organizations regarding the BN reveals how they each tried to negotiate several strategic dilemmas while trying to present a unified front to the government. These dilemmas included strategizing in ways that both advance the professional interest of individual nurses (practical gender needs) and advance their collective interests (strategic gender needs). In terms of choosing the "right" strategy, by proposing the BN, NANB was trying to think critically about the professional situation of nurses, and their inability to control their work priorities. NANB obviously thought that an integral part of their struggle to influence the ability of nurses to nurse, and thus their work conditions (and maybe their strategic gender interests), was to increase their professional status. The BN was important if only because it involved working toward legitimizing nursing skills and knowledge, and toward recognizing and appropriately valuing their competence as skilled workers. This might then affect their ability to have their claims taken seriously because it is an attempt to explicitly challenge assumptions about the work nurses do.

Nursing work has been considered to be "the product of abilities which are natural or innate ... rather than something that requires skill or knowledge" (Stelling 1994: 205). As Lorraine Code (1991) argues, because nursing work is considered private (and unproductive), it is thus undervalued, although it is performed in the public sphere. Nurses are considered selfless workers, performing a "labour of love," reproductive and not productive work that lots of women do free in the home. This type of caring work is not considered to involve essential activities with important decision-making attached (such as activities performed by physicians, for example, to diagnose, treat, and cure). It is important that these assumptions about "women's work" be challenged—especially during neoliberal restructuring.

Assumptions about nursing being "women's work" underlie neoliberal restructuring, which seeks to measure and rationalize services to achieve cost-efficient health care. The rationalization process is facilitated by assumptions that nursing work (especially the caring work) does not necessarily require training to learn the required skills and knowledge. Under neoliberal restructuring, this construction of certain types of work as domestic, familial, unskilled activity has allowed some of it to be devolved as unpaid, voluntary work to women in the home (Armstrong 1994: 99). It has also meant that nurses' nursing work has been largely devalued, while they are left doing more non-nursing work such as housekeeping. Hospitals take advantage of nurses' commitment and around-the-clock care of patients and assume that nurses will do non-nursing tasks to ensure their patients' well-being (Stelling 1994: 213). It was even reported that the New Brunswick government was substituting less experienced and qualified workers where possible, changing job classifications and then rehiring nurses in non-nursing positions (Atkinson 1992). Indeed, in 1994 the New Brunswick government proposed eliminating the word "nursing" in nurses' job descriptions (Hoyt-Magee 1994: 31). Although the government did not succeed, this attempt is significant and illustrates the lack of value placed on what it means to nurse in the province. The government wanted to replace references to nursing with generic terms, thus demobilizing organized nurses' struggle to resist and influence restructuring by undermining the very foundation of their claims.

Organized nursing wanted to ensure that nurses would have more control over their work and be more able to determine their work priorities. One difficulty with making proposals was negotiating both the neoliberal economic discourse and the dominant biomedical model of the health system favouring physicians' dominance. As Code insightfully argues, while nurses are not all or completely disempowered, the "power/knowledge arrangements of professional medicine legitimate an uneven distribution of speaking and knowing positions that usually works to contain knowledgeable practice of nurses within stereotypical female roles" (1991: 245). While the New Brunswick government agreed to the BN, the decision probably had more to do with the Association's argument that the BN-trained nurses were cheaper than diploma-nurses to educate (NANB 1991: 16-17). In addition, the association argued that BN-trained nurses could better respond to the need for professionals who have broad-based knowledge and portable skills, a need that increases as "economics and outcome oriented service provision continue to drive decision-making in health care" (NANB 1993: 3). NANB positioned BN-trained nurses as the "cheaper" alternative to physicians, thus legitimizing the importance of cost (efficiency) as the driving force behind restructuring.

Arguably, NANB was strategically positioning itself and nurses to be heard. It recognized that previous health policy had been dominated by discursive elements that emphasized curing and clinical research as "evidence" for making decisions, but that current neoliberal economic discourse privileges managers and economists, and those able to provide evidence of cost-efficiency (or cost-saving more specifically). This positioning is problematic insofar as cost-efficiency is a relative valuation and thus they are forced into a position to argue that nurses could provide more cost-efficient primary health care than doctors, which then reinforces the territorial battles between them. As in other provinces, making a cost-efficient argument may only mean increasing the nurses' responsibility and workload, but not their authority, while they are still held accountable for cost-efficient patient care and budget cuts (Armstrong 1993: 45-46). Trying to be strategically effective by focussing more on becoming (cost-efficient) primary health caregivers who share certain "scientific" competencies and skills with physicians may only have left nurses doing more non-nursing work.

Valuing Their Shared Competence, Sacrificing their Ability to Nurse?

Another key component to implementing PHC so that nurses could assume a greater role in the health care system was to propose that a shared-competence model should be used for assessing the best primary care giver. Using this model, which professional is assigned responsibility depends on where the care is given (health centre, extra mural hospital program, etc.), which is facilitated by physicians and nurses working in shared practice in certain settings. In contrast to a functional-team concept, a shared compe-tence-based model would recognize that both nurses and physicians have distinct responsibilities but that their responsibilities sometimes overlap in areas where both may have the same expertise and skill (NRAC 1993).

The key shared competencies that nurses could perform when delivering primary health care included doing the initial assessment, making referrals, and in certain contexts performing admittance and discharge (NRAC 1993: 6). However, these competencies are done by physicians and while there has been some shifting of medical practices to nurses, the changes to the hierarchical relationship have not been significant enough. As stated by NANB such significant changes have been thwarted by "powerful physician lobbies which retain the physician as the major point of entry to care and limit access to the system" (1988: 8). Indeed, in response to nurses' PHC proposal, the New Brunswick Medical Society (NBMS) stated outright that it "must object to the suggestion that primary nurses serve as the point of contact for patients" (NBMS 1990: 6). This is significant because a key selling points of organized nurses' PHC proposal was that it offered multiple access[10] points and alternative providers.

The New Brunswick government has set up programs[11] that indicate some willingness to enhance the role of nurses and that embody PHC principles. While nurses do have more autonomy and authority in these programs, functions have not been formally transferred to nurses, and nurses' increased competence has not been formally recognized. The situation for nurses within these programs is in line with what the research has shown regarding other governments: more often than not, any attempts to formally rationalize the delegation of functions to nurses have been thwarted because governments have been hesitant to override decisions of professional regulatory bodies in an area of functional authority (in this case physicians) (Touhy 1986). The delegation of functions is on a case-by-case basis and what might apply in one setting may not in another.[12] As one NANB executive member described, in their campaign to increase their status nurses are "playing a cautious political game" (Grove 1991: 194). This political game leaves nurses in a precarious position for advancing their proposal to use a shared competence-based model for health and human resource planning.

Working collaboratively according to a competence-based model entails recognizing and acknowledging areas of shared competence instead of solidifying professional and disciplinary boundaries. In a time of restructuring, no group feels secure in its position. As a result, while this may be a good time to forge alliances, it is also a time when tensions are the highest between and among these groups. Only those who are secure in their positions can move to the type of cooperation advocated in a shared competence-based model. Nurses do not appear secure nor have they seen their security increased under restructuring, though they had choices to make about how best to secure their ability to nurse.

Organized nursing had choices to make about what evidence and arguments they should use to have their claims legitimized. In trying to negotiate the government's construction of health system restructuring and nursing work, organized nurses may have offered the government an opportunity to exploit their tasks, expanding them, but not recognizing or appropriately valuing their distinct competencies. These organizations did not want to continue to be marginalized by naming caring as what distinguishes their profession, but neither did they want to deny what their work entails. Demanding that caring be (re)valued would go against the managerial rationalization of the profession and government's attempts to proletarianize (McPherson 1996: 262). However, Fisher argues that basing their claims on caring contributes to the glorification of the home (domestic sphere) and women's roles, and reinforces stereotypes about the nature of gender differences that led many to believe in the biological essentialist arguments about women's natural nurturing ability to take care of others (1994: 301). Fisher further contends that the best strategy for organized nursing would be to base its struggles on advancing PHC and community-based care.

Nurses should have been able to base their claims on their clinical knowledge (which has a scientific knowledge base), but also on their subjective knowing and close front-line, around-the-clock relationship with patients. However, the latter type of knowledge has been generally judged incompatible with scientific standards of inquiry, and has resulted in the denial of their expertise (Allen and Jensen 1996: 96-98). Indeed, knowledge claims that have historically been associated with femininity (and with nursing) such as emotion, connection, practicality, and sensitivity have not been recognized as expert (Code 1991).[13] What was their best strategy considering these dilemmas?

Reconceptualizing Organized Nurses' Strategic Dilemmas

If we were to employ the two conceptual frameworks (practical and strategic gender needs; problem-solving and critical-thinking) to classify the choices made by these organizations, we could conclude that the professional association tended more toward solving nurses' strategic gender needs, such as proposing a Bachelor of Nursing as sole entry to practice, whereas the union tended to respond to more practical gender needs such as wages. There was some concern (expressed by the union and some nurse members) that resources might have been better spent addressing their practical gender needs than achieving the BN standard. These practical needs could have been addressed in terms of day-to-day working conditions with problem-solving solutions such as pushing the government to hire more nurses or to convert some casual positions to full-time permanent ones. The nature of the union is such that it favours more problem-solving approaches because the solutions are often felt immediately. The hesitation of the union to embrace a more critical-thinking strategy may point to the reason many groups are hesitant to embrace critical-thinking strategies and debates about knowledge—they are seen as apolitical and paralyzing as they divert resources away from organizing and reacting to the threat urgently posed by restructuring.[14]

The limitation of a stark dualistic distinction to understanding the strategic dilemmas faced by these organizations leaves out the creative tensions between the two and thus between the union and the professional association. What is more important, such distinctions do not allow for the possibility that a strategy can involve both approaches: a problem-solving approach answering to women's practical needs can also involve critical-thinking and address women's strategic needs. Should nursing organizations have concentrated on using a problem-solving approach favored by the union to propose solutions or was the BN (and a critical-thinking approach) more useful? I would argue that neither alone is preferable, that instead we need to challenge such dualistic understanding.

The dualistic conceptualization of these strategies would suggest that the union may only help nurses to cope better in their roles instead of work-ing to transform the unequal gender relations that circumscribe these roles. In contrast, using this framework to achieve a more systemic analysis of nurses' subordination would lead to a critical-thinking strategy that responds to their strategic gender needs. The BN and the PHC proposals may be classified as such because they could affect nurses' collective empowerment as they challenge both the way health professionals are currently organized and utilized, and ultimately systemic hierarchical inequities. I would argue that to best approach the strategic dilemmas of the nursing organizations we need to reconceptualize such dualistic approaches, so as to understand why their best strategy was to address nurses' practical gender needs strategically and yet not sacrifice a critical-thinking approach for a problem-solving one. The best strategy is one that tries to reconcile these dualisms while maintaining the creative tensions between them, which is what both nursing organizations tried to do together. The issues raised regarding educational/professional standards point to the need for a better understanding of the interconnections between problem-solving and critical-thinking solutions and between practical and strategic gender needs. Developing strategies to respond to nurses' needs must include a better understanding of the interconnections between nurses' professional concerns about education credentials, and those that the union focuses more on—nurses' concerns about everyday work conditions (e.g. hours, wages, staffing).

A nuanced understanding of strategic dilemmas should recognize that women's immediate (practical gender) needs are interconnected with their strategic needs and that a problem-solving approach is not so easily distin-guished from a critical-thinking one because they can work together. Applied to organized nurses' strategies, PHC was an important proposal because it challenged the biomedical-model and the social-political power relations and values that underlie the health system. However, a problem-solving approach and strategy can also work to change the way nursing work (e.g. caring) is marginalized and the way the system is organized in a rigid, hierarchical fashion. As I have shown here, those strategies that do not appear to address strategic gender needs or that do not appear to challenge unequal gender relations are often the most successful ones. Such strategies open the door to the possibility of transformative changes that other strategies might have precluded. Therefore, it was important that organized nurses not only resisted the immediate negative effects of health system restructuring on nurses, but that they tried to influence its direction.

Conclusion

At the edge of the millennium, feminists can learn from nurses' organizations' attempts to influence restructuring while resisting its negative impact on their profession. Had they only resisted restructuring they may not have had the opportunity to raise the questions they did in demanding such substantial changes to the health care delivery system. Organized nurses argued that the system will need to be reoriented toward PHC for it to be more effective and strategically positioned nurses as an underutilized resource. In making the proposals they did, nursing organizations were raising fundamental questions about what our health care priorities should be in the new millennium.

Nurses' organizations realized quickly that in their attempts to reduce health care costs and meet increasing demands for improved care, governments must consider options that under different circumstances they might have ignored. However, as shown here, one of the risks of intervening in any policy process is that disjunctures often occur between proposing alternatives and having them instituted. This is especially the case when the government's reform agenda is about cost-cutting, which has attacked the very values that underlie the kind of care that nurses provide. Health system restructuring has assumed that nurses' commitment to take care of their patients will ensure that they will fill any gaps left by short term cost-cutting measures. Similarly, neoliberal economic restructuring has assumed that women's commitment to take care of their family and their community will ensure the same.

A focus on organized nursing and health system restructuring provides a reading of health system reform and health policy decision-making from a location of nursing as "women's work." As Mohanty argues, to study women's work is to study "the ideological construction of jobs and tasks in terms of notions of femininity, domesticity, (hetero)sexuality, and racial and cultural stereotypes" (1997: 6). Nursing organizations were struggling against the dominant view that their members are just unskilled labourers, whose "feminine" skills are most appropriate in the home. From their struggles we learned that nursing shapes and is shaped by structures of power, and resource distribution in the health system and by ways of knowing.

Underlying my examination of organized nursing was the premise that different forms of knowledge result in the mobilization of different forms of change (Wainwright 1994). However, I am not calling for an uncritical acceptance of nurses' knowledge claims or indeed those of other marginalized groups. Rather, we need to democratize the way the state learns about problems and solutions and to democratize larger governance processes, which would involve recognizing the value in democratizing knowledge. Democratizing knowledge means sharing different sources of knowledge to stimulate further analysis, explain problems, and find ways to change (Wainwright 1994). Admittedly, we have yet to effectively theorize what democratization of knowledge means in practice. Ultimately, women need to be empowered to interpret their own health needs according to the complexities of their roles as beneficiaries, workers, and paid and unpaid caregivers in the system (Fraser 1989).

Learning from the interventions of these organizations during restructuring and the effect this process has had on nursing, we are cautioned against relying uncritically on the state or one institution to achieve our goals for the new millennium. In Bakker and Elson's words, "we need to understand the positive opportunities for equality and the negative implications of restructuring for inequality"(1998: 306). For nurses and others who do "women's work" such opportunities depend on how one is positioned socially, economically and politically, and the value or undervalue attributed to the kind of skills and knowledge required to do the work. In the long term, we need to work together to make changes to the webs of power that sustain gender inequality, and to who and what should be involved in making decisions about our social needs.

My dissertation research contributed to this article and as such I wish to acknowledge the financial support for the larger project by the Ontario and New Brunswick governments for the Ontario Graduate Scholarship and New BrunswickWomen's Doctoral Scholarship, as well as the Maritime Centre of Excellence for Women's Health and the O'Brien Foundation. I want to thank my supervisor Dr. Isabella Bakker, and Kate Bezanson, Krista Hunt, Melanie Stewart Millar, and Dr. Leah Vosko for their helpful comments on previous drafts.

[1]I use governance to indicate that while this article concentrates on govern-

ment policy, the role of "private" actors such as nurses will only increase as powers are devolved from governments onto communities and more informal structures and interests. As such, the problems of the new millennium will increasingly need to be collectively solved. Therefore, the term recognizes that government is but one instrument of "public" governance.

[2]Most gains in gender equality in employment (the public service was an important unionized workplace for many women), pay equity, childcare, education, and retraining have stalled since the 1970s and some have been lost since the 1980s (Brodie 1995: 20).

[3]Professionalization involves attaining (social) authority and workplace autonomy, increased legitimation and status of their distinct body of knowledge (McPherson 1996: 6-7). In contrast, proletarianization refers to the intensification of the pace of work, a rigid hierarchical division of labor and rationalization of the work process towards an assembly-line, factory production type of workplace (McPherson 1996: 8).

[4]These key concepts were first coined by Caroline Moser (1989).

[5]The World Health Organization (WHO) defines PHC as "essential health care made universally accessible to individuals and families in the community, by means acceptable to them, and through their full participation and at a cost the community and province can afford" (WHO, 1978, cited in NANB 1991a: 2).

[6]Nurses would become primary care givers in such settings as the extra-mural hospital programme or community health centres.

[7]When this proposal was made, a RN qualification in the province could be obtained from five colleges offering a two-year diploma in nursing, or from two universities offering a four-year Bachelor of Nursing. The BN as sole entry to practice would eliminate the college diploma program.

[8]For a summary of arguments for and against the BN see Briant and Steward (1981). See also Kerr and MacPhail (1996).

[9]For more detail on the disagreement see Hoyt-Magee (1994: 30).

[10]The possibility does exist to open the system up to nurses and allow them to bill for their services. It was the Canadian Nurses Association's lobby in 1984 that changed the wording in the Canada Health Act regarding remuneration from "medical practitioner" to "health care practitioner." The purpose of the lobby was to acknowledge all such practitioners as equal and signal redirection from physician and hospital dominance. Although, no province has moved to allow nurses to bill for their services, the potential exists. Recognizing the importance of this, the nursing organizations in New Brunswick have argued that at least in the shared settings physicians be paid by salary just like nurses.

This may be an easier fight than the fight to allow nurses to bill medicare.
[11]My goal for this article is not to assess the success of such programs including the Extra Mural Hospital, Seniors Singly Entry Point Program, and pilot Community Health Centre, as space does not permit it, but rather to consider the role of nurses in them.

[12]New Brunswick Medical Society (NBMS) and the NANB have maintained a joint committee on the delegation of medical procedures for eight to ten years now (NBMS 1990).

[13]The insights drawn from Code (1991) are mainly from Chapter Six in which she discusses the 1984 Grange Inquiry into infant deaths from cardiac arrest at Toronto's Hospital for Sick Children, which some feminists have called a "witch hunt" aimed at nurses. See also Elaine Buckley Day (1997).

[14]Janet Conway (1999) discusses the distinction in her analysis of the Metro Network for Social Justice.

Appendix A

Profile of Nursing in New Brunswick

Employment Status, Casualization and Part-Time:

- Increase in casual employment for all RNs: From 13% in 1990 to 18% in 1996
- Dramatic increase in casual employment for RNs under the age of 25: 11%, 1990 to 96%, 1996
- 80% of nurses report dissatisfaction with their employment status
- 77% of RNs under 25 work 30 hours or less, up from 8% in 1990
- New RNs can expect to work as casuals for anywhere from six to eight years.

Demographics:

- Decrease in the number of new RN graduates remaining in the province (after 1 year); 85% in 1991 to 54% in 1997
- Within 10 years, 45% of all RNs will be over 50 years of age

Occupational Health and Safety Concerns:

- Increase in patient acuity, workload and responsibilities, and decrease in support and resources
- Increase in abuse, violence, workplace stress and disabilities

Christine Saulnier

Quality of Worklife Issues:
- Face instability in their work environment (with staff turnover, casualization, etc.)
- Low staff morale, decrease in self-esteem, an increase in the level of stress
- Climate of uncertainty due to constant, rapid and radical change; lead to role confusion

Information From Nursing Resource Advisory Committee, 1993, and 1997.

References

Allen, M. N. and L. A. Jensen. "Knowledge Development in Nursing." *Concepts in Canadian Nursing.* Eds. J. Kerr and J. MacPhail. St Louis, Miss.: Mosby, 1996.

Armstrong, P. "Closer to Home: More Work for Women." *Take Care: Warning Signals for Canada's Health System.* Eds. P. and H. Armstrong, J. Choinier, G. Feldberg and J. White. Toronto: Garamond Press, 1994. 95-110.

Armstrong, P. "Women's Health Care Work: Nursing in Context." *Vital Signs: Nursing in Transition.* Eds. P. Armstrong, J. Choiniere, and E. Day. Toronto: Garamond Press, 1993. 17-58.

Armstrong, P. and H. Armstrong. *Wasting Away: The Undermining of Canadian Health Care.* Toronto: Oxford University Press, 1996.

Bakker, I., ed. *Rethinking Restructuring: Gender and Change in Canada.* Toronto: University of Toronto Press, 1996.

Bakker, I. and D. Elson. "Towards Engendering Budgets." *Alternative Federal Budget Papers 1998.* Ottawa, Canadian Centre for Policy Alternatives and Choices, 1998. 297-324.

Briant, N. J. and J. Steward. "The BN as Entry into the Profession, Yes or No?" *InfoNursing* 12 (5)(1981): 14-18.

Brodie, J. *Politics on the Margins: Restructuring and the Canadian Women's Movement.* Halifax: Fernwood, 1995.

Code, L. *What Can She Know? Feminist Theory and the Construction of Knowledge.* Ithaca: Cornell University Press, 1991.

Conway, Janet. *Knowledge, Power, Organization: Social Justice Coalitions at a Crossroads.* Occastional Paper No. 1. Community Social Planning Council of Toronto, October 1999.

Day, Elaine Buckley. "A Twentieth Century Witch Hunt: A Feminist Critique of the Grange Royal Commission into Deaths at the Hospital for Sick Children." *Studies in Political Economy* 24 (Autumn 1997): 13-39.

DeMont, J. "Fast Frank: How New Brunswick's Premier Turned his Province into Canada's Social Laboratory." *Macleans*. April 11, 1994: 22-28.

Fisher, S. "Is Care a Remedy? The Case of Nurse Practitioners." *Reframing Women's Health: Multidisciplinary Research and Practice*. Ed. A. J. Dan. London: Sage, 1994.

Fraser, N. *Unruly Practices: Power, Discourse, and Gender in Contemporary Social Theory*. Minneapolis: University of Minnesota, 1989.

Gill, S. "Epistemology, Ontology, and the 'Italian School'." *Gramsci, Historical Materialism and International Relations*. Ed. Stephen Gill. New York: Cambridge University Press, 1993. 21-48.

Grove, S. *Who Cares? The Crisis in Canadian Nursing*. Toronto: McClelland and Stewart Inc., 1991.

Hoyt-Magee, A. *The Strength of One: A History of the New Brunswick Nurses Union*. Fredericton: New Brunswick Nursing Union, 1994.

Keddy, B., D. Denney, F. Gregor, and S. Foster. *Theorizing About the Gendered Nature of "Nurses' Work/Womens' Work" During the Era of Health Care "Reform": Nova Scotia and British Columbia Nurses Tell their Stories*. Vancouver: University of British Columbia, Centre for Research in Women's Studies and Gender Relations, 1998.

Kerr, J. and J. MacPhail. "The Changing Face of Nursing Education in Canada." *Concepts in Canadian Nursing*. Eds. J. Kerr and J. MacPhail. St Louis, Miss.: Mosby, 1996.

McPherson, K. *Bedside Matters: The Transformation of Canadian Nursing 1900-1990*. Toronto: Oxford University Press, 1996.

Mohanty, C. T. "Women workers and Capitalist Scripts: Ideologies of Domination, Common Interests and the Politics of Solidarity." *Feminist Geneologies, Colonial Legacies, Democratic Futures*. Eds. Alexander and Mohanty. New York: Routledge, 1997. 3-29.

Moser, Caroline O. N. "Gender Planning in the Third World: Meeting Practical and Strategic Gender Needs." *World Development* 17(1)(1989): 1799-1825.

Moser, Caroline O. N., A. Tornquvist and B. van Bronkhorst. *Mainstreaming Gender and Development in the World Bank: Progress and Recommendations*. Washington, D.C.: The World Bank, 1999.

Parsons, W. *Public Policy: An Introduction to the Theory and Practice of Policy Analysis*. Parsons-Brookfield, Vermont: Edward Elgar, 1995.

Christine Saulnier

Stelling, J. "Nursing Metaphors: Reflections on the Meaning of Time." *Women, Medicine and Health*. Eds. B. Singh Bolaria and R. Bolaria. Halifax: Fernwood, 1994. 205-271.

Touhy, C. "Conflict and Accomodation in the Canadian Health Care System." *Medicare at Maturity*. Eds. R. Evans *et al.* Calgary: University of Calgary Press, 1986. 393-434.

Wainright, H. *Arguments for a New Left: Answering the Free-Market Right*. Oxford: Blackwell, 1994.

Primary Documents

Atkinson, A. *Executive Director's Annual Report. Info Nursing Supplement*. 1992.

Auffrey, L. *Executive Director's Annual Report. Info Nursing Supplement*. 1994.

New Brunswick Medical Society (NBMS). *Response to the Report and Recommendations of the Commission on Selected Health Care Programs*. Frederiction: Author. 1990.

New Brunswick Nurses Union (NBNU). *Health: Too Precious to Gamble With!* Fredericton: Author. 1994.

Nurses Association of New Brunswick (NANB) *Position Statement on Primary Health Care*. Fredericton: Author. 1996.

Nurses Association of New Brunswick (NANB). *The Role of the Nurse*. Fredericton: Author. 1993.

Nurses Association of New Brunswick (NANB). *Health Care Reform, Health 2000: Background Paper Prepared for Lobby Campaign on Health Care Reform and Future Education for Nurses*. Fredericton: Author. 1991.

Nurses Association of New Brunswick (NANB). *Response to the Premier's Council on Health Strategy's Draft Report on Health Promotion and Prevention Issues*. Fredericton: Author. 1991a.

Nurses Association of New Brunswick (NANB). *Presentation on Concerns of Nurses in New Brunswick to the Nursing Human Resources Advisory Committee*. Fredericton: Author. 1988.

Nursing Resources Advisory Committee (NRAC) *Nursing Resource Challenges; Recruitment and Retention of Nursing Service Providers*. Fredericton: Department of Community and Health Services, Government of New Brunswick. 1997.

Nursing Resources Advisory Committee (NRAC) *Report on the Nursing Service and Resource Management in New Brunswick*. Fredericton: Department of Community and Health Services, Government of New Brunswick. 1993.

Section II:
Contesting Foundations

How Women Are Defined (by the Goddess?)
A Re-examination of Carol Christ's Reflections

Chris Klassen

As we stand on the edge of the millennium the future seems wide-open, full of possibility and calling for new voices, new inspiration and new direction. This is true for all areas of feminist theory and scholarship, but it is particularly true for feminist spirituality and thealogy (the study of female divinity). This is an age of religious creation. Large numbers of women are leaving traditional religions, if they have not already done so, to walk spiritual paths of their own devising. Some become Witches. Some become worshippers of specific Goddesses. Some resist definitions. What is common to many of these women is a focus on Goddess imagery as a way of shaping their feminist identities.

With all the potential of the future it is sometimes tempting to completely let go of the past. However, to do so would be a mistake. Those who have come before us have placed the groundwork from which we build today. Sometimes there is some "unbuilding" to do first to make sure our own constructions are not laid on shaky ground. Strengthening our foundations by re-examining the thoughts and ideas of previous scholars is necessary in the process of moving into the future.

An important foundational thinker to re-examine in feminist thealogy is Carol Christ. Christ began her career as a Christian theologian. Her journey away from Christianity to Goddess religion has been inspirational to many women. Rita Gross, in *Feminism and Religion*, classifies Christ as one of "the two most eloquent [revolutionary] feminists" in the realm of religion and theo(a)logy, along with Mary Daly. Christ's journey has motivated her to theorize about the role religious symbolism can hold in developing feminist consciousness. In her influential essay "Why Women Need the Goddess: Phenomenological, Psychological, and Political Reflections" Christ asserts, "[b]ecause religion has such a compelling hold on the deep psyches of so many people, feminists cannot afford to leave it in the hands of the father" (1979: 274). Feminists should not ignore the continuing influence of religious symbolism in most people's lives, whether it be a conscious or unconscious influence. Rather, says Christ, feminists should work to shape this symbolism in ways that reflect women's lived experiences, and thus empower women in their everyday lives.

Because she has been so influential to so many women—scholars and nonscholars alike—Christ's foundational work must be re-examined to determine what is useful to build on and what needs to be "unbuilt" first. This paper engages in that re-examination by exploring the symbolism Christ develops, along with her use of the categories of "woman" and "female"—categories which I will show Christ uses in problematic ways. Christ claims that Goddess imagery counters the false dualisms of patriarchy. If this is the case, it would seem necessary that this imagery address the dualism of male-female and its patriarchal construction around reproduction. Yet in "Why Women Need the Goddess" Christ tends to maintain this dualism by using the categories of "woman" and "female" to continue to identify females according to reproductive roles. Furthermore, her early uses of "woman" and "female" tend toward a universalizing which does not take into account differences among women, such as sexuality and race. Because "Why Women Need the Goddess" is an early piece of thealogy, I also examine a later work, *Rebirth of the Goddess* (1997), in order to see how Christ's use of these problematic categories has progressed and where it still needs improvement. Ultimately, I ask how a reworking of these categories away from patriarchal dualisms affects the use of Goddess symbolism, and conversely how Goddess symbolism maintains and/ or challenges the categories of "woman" and "female," thus challenging the dualistic construction of male-female and the universalizing of womanhood. These questions are necessary in order to begin thinking about the future of Goddess imagery as a tool for feminist theory and the construction of feminist spiritual identities.

Christ begins her discussion of the importance of Goddess imagery for feminist thealogy in "Why Women Need the Goddess" where she draws on Clifford Geertz's notion of religion as a system of symbols to analyze the psychological and political effects of the contemporary Goddess religion. Geertz held that religious symbols create psychological moods which lead to social and political motivations. These motivations shape and maintain social and political realities, which in turn inform religious symbols. Keeping this in mind, Christ uses her essay to begin a phenomenological discussion of the feminist call for a rejection of patriarchal religious symbolism (such as the Father God and the male saviour Jesus found within Christianity). In addition, she explores how the symbol of the Goddess creates psychological moods which motivate woman-friendly social and political realities.

There are four aspects of the symbol of the Goddess which Christ focuses on. First Christ shows how the symbol of the Goddess affirms female power. She speaks of this power as beneficent and independent in contrast to the patriarchal construction of female power as inferior and dangerous (1979: 277). Christ then demonstrates how western patriarchal societies and cultures denigrate the female body through constructing menstruation as a "curse," childbirth as pathological and ageing women as ugly, evil "hags." Goddess symbolism on the other hand reinforces the sacredness of the female body and life-cycles (1979: 279). Her third point laments the fact that in patriarchal societies women are expected to be dependent on men and to subordinate their wills to those of their fathers, brothers, husbands, sons. The symbol of the Goddess not only allows women to think for themselves but constructs female will as powerful through ritual magic (1979: 282).[1] In her final point, Christ refers back to Virginia Woolf's discussion in *A Room of One's Own* of the relationships between women (or the lack thereof) in fiction. ("Chloe liked Olivia.") Patriarchy constructs women only in relation to men thus ignoring women's relationships. Goddess symbolism brings these relationships to the forefront, recognizing them as important and as sacred—particularly the mother-daughter relationship (1979: 285).

In *Rebirth of the Goddess*, Christ provides a systematic thealogy which follows the traditional theological model of addressing the nature of deity, the universe, humanity, and ethics. Her concern in this work is to, on the one hand, provide a model for understanding Goddess worship as a full-fledged religion, and on the other hand, demonstrate how different Goddess religion is from traditional, patriarchal religion. In this later work, Christ takes up many of the same ideas about Goddess symbolism as in "Why Women Need the Goddess," though they are tempered by almost twenty years of experience and interaction with other feminist thealogians and Goddess worshippers.

Christ's critique of patriarchal religions, in both works, is significant in its direct assault on God imagery without rejecting religion itself. She points out that:

> [R]eligions centered on the worship of a male God create "moods" and "motivations" that keep women in a state of psychological dependence on men and male authority, while at the same legitimating the *political* and *social* authority of fathers and sons in the institutions of society. (1979: 275)

The idea that the sex and/or gender of one's deity is irrelevant to one's lived experience, is preposterous to Christ. Deity, for her, is a model for humanity. The characteristics given to a male God will be transferred also to male humans and denied to female humans when male and female are constructed as binary opposites. While some feminists might see this as a good reason to do away with religion altogether, Christ sees the importance of religious symbolism for psychological and political reasons. She maintains that symbols need to be replaced, not just rejected. According to Christ if we merely reject patriarchal religious symbolism without putting something else in its place we will ultimately revert back to it in times of need, such as death and illness, thus maintaining the cycle of moods and motivations. The solution, Christ suggests, is Goddess imagery. She writes, "the Goddess is woman whole in herself. She speaks to us of a power that is our birthright" (1997: 8). Women, she says, need to replace the Father God with a Goddess—thus creating a cycle of moods and motivations which are woman-centred.

It is undeniable that many women have found Goddess symbolism to be empowering. They have found within it affirmations of their abilities, bodies, thoughts, relationships, and spiritualities—as women; experiences they were denied in patriarchal religion. However, if the developing Goddess religion is to be empowering for all women, it is important to ask what it means to talk about *female* power, the *female* body, the *female* will and *women's* bonds and heritage. How are women, and the female, being defined here?

To explore what Christ means when she talks of women and females I will begin with her early account of women's identity within patriarchal religions. In a system of patriarchal religious symbols, Christ points out that a woman

> may see herself as like God (created in the image of God) only by denying her own sexual identity and affirming God's transcendence of sexual identity. But she can never have the experience that is freely available to every man and boy in her culture, of having her full sexual identity affirmed as being in the image and likeness of God. (1979: 275)

There is an implication in this statement that sexual identity[2] is prior to the construction of patriarchal religious symbolism. A woman has "her own sexual identity" which is either affirmed or denied by society but does not seem to be shaped by it. And this sexual identity is inherently different from that of "*every man and boy*" (emphasis added).[3] Thus we get the sense here that Christ is assuming two sexual identities that are essential and irreducible.

Christ is confirming what Judith Butler laments in *Bodies that Matter*:

> It has seemed to many, I think, that in order for feminism to proceed as a critical practice, it must ground itself in the sexed specificity of the female body. Even as the category of sex is always reinscribed as gender, that sex must still be presumed as the irreducible point of departure for the various cultural constructions it has come to bear. (1993: 28)

Though feminists are insistent on questioning the nature of gender—how women and men are to act, relate to others, present themselves in the world—sex is assumed as a given. In the words of Suzanne J. Kessler and Wendy McKenna, "Most people would admit that the cultural trappings of males and females have varied over place and time, but that nevertheless, there is something essentially male and something essentially female" (1978: 1). In "Why Women Need the Goddess," Christ is drawing on this understanding of the essential nature of being female; "sexual identity" is a given. But Butler claims that the body cannot be seen as prior to discourse, as unconstructed. It is constructed by a gendered matrix. To see the sexed body as irreducible reinforces this gendered matrix thus reducing the effectiveness of feminist discourses. In other words, the body cannot be conceptualized outside of social constructions. If these social constructions already maintain a gendered opposition, the body will be understood as naturally fitting into such a dualism. We perceive bodies to be sexed as either male or female, with no other options, because we conceptualize the body through a gendered matrix. If feminists like Christ are working to change social and religious realities they must work to reconceptualize the body. To do this they must rethink the construction of a male-female dualism, not only to disrupt notions of gender (masculinity and femininity), but also to disrupt notions of essential "biological" sex.

The essential nature of sex and/or sexual identity is carried through Christ's discussion of Goddess symbolism. Nowhere does she inform us of what makes female power, or female will, etc., *female* (in contrast to male power, male will), other than that they are motivations and actions of a female body. Of course this brings us to the question of what constitutes a female body. For Christ, it seems to be the ability to menstruate and give birth. She writes, "because of women's unique position as menstruants, birth-givers, and those who have traditionally cared for the young and the dying, women's connection to the body, nature, and this world has been obvious" (1979: 279). Therefore the symbol of the Goddess, as a divine female body, brings the body, nature, the earth, and women into the realm of the sacred.[4] The importance of resacralizing the physical and that which has been deemed "feminine" is important, but it bears asking why Christ does not question the *obviousness* of this connection. This is a connection which has been constructed through patriarchal discourses around dualism and polarities, a connection which Elizabeth Grosz locates in misogynist thought. Grosz writes:

> [T]he coding of femininity with corporeality in effect leaves men free to inhabit what they (falsely) believe is a purely conceptual order while at the same time enabling them to satisfy their (sometimes disavowed) need for corporeal contact through their access to women's bodies and services. (1994: 14)

Understanding women as obviously connected to the body and nature (as a necessary aspect of their femaleness) reinforces the binary between mind and body, and its gendered associations. Must reinscribing value onto the physical and the female involve a reinforcement of their "obvious" connection (other than the ideological connection of their devaluing—which is the very thing being opposed)? Similarly, must revaluing menstruation and birth reduce the female body to *primarily* a menstruant and/or birth-giver? It seems that for Christ what makes a body female is its reproductive capacities and functions. This is reinforced in her discussion of women's relationships where she focuses on the mother-daughter bond as opposed to that of lovers or friends or co-workers.[5] But Christ does not address women who do not menstruate or cannot (or choose not to) give birth. Are their bodies less female than those who do menstruate and give birth? How are their bodies affirmed by the symbol of the Goddess?

There is potential in Christ's later work to move beyond this male-female dichotomy which essentializes sex (or at least a recognition that the dichotomy is a construction). In the preface to *Rebirth of the Goddess*, Christ calls us to think holistically in order to transform the dualisms which have been so damaging. "The return of the Goddess inspires us to hope that we can heal the deep rifts between women and men, between "man" and nature and between "God" and the world, that have shaped our western view of reality for too long" (1997: iii). But the potential of this statement does not become a reality as later on in the book she claims that "sexual differentiation is one of the obvious facts of our bodily existence. [...] women have breasts, vaginas, ovaries, and uteruses, while men have penises and testes" (1997: 148). Christ is still asserting here that there are two sexes—male and female—and they are defined by their reproductive organs.

In her response to those who have labelled her essentialist, Christ argues that a thealogy which begins at women's lived experiences must address birth-giving and nurturing as "the physical realities of most women's lives in every existing culture of the world" (1997: 92). I am not arguing against the realities of many women's lives, but it is important to move beyond the reproductive when basing feminist thealogy or theory on women's lived experiences. Thus when Christ asks, "wouldn't it be better off if our symbols and theories acknowledge the creative powers *inherent* in the female body and in the nurturing of life?" (1997: 93, [emphasis added]), I have to ask which women are being left out of this discussion?

Christ also does not address how queer sexualities may affect one's femaleness. Butler writes, "Gender norms operate by requiring the embodi-ment of certain ideals of femininity and masculinity, ones that are almost always related to the idealization of the heterosexual bond" (231-232). Because Christ does not address sex as a construction, she maintains the gendered matrix which upholds heterosexuality as the norm. Thus, in "Why Women Need the Goddess," Christ does not leave any room for ambiguous sex identities. For example, does a butch lesbian, who presents herself as masculine yet has breasts and a vagina, have a female (feminine?) sexual identity? Is a preoperative male-to-female transsexual who looks and acts like a woman (whatever that may be) but has a penis, considered female? Does she have female power? Female will? Or does her lack of menstruating or birth-giving ability disqualify her? These are questions which Christ's theories leave no room to ask.

While in *Rebirth of the Goddess* Christ does begin to recognize the possibilities of ambiguous sexual identities (1997: 149), it is unclear how she fits these "individuals" into the discussion of "obvious (or 'primary') biological sex differences" (1997: 148). Through her very use of the term "individuals" Christ does not allow her analysis to unsettle "the assertion of primary sexual differences" (1997: 149). She, in fact, sets up sexually ambiguous "individuals" as merely examples of "deviants" outside the "norm." Even though she allows that the existence of the ambiguous individuals complicates the assertion of sex difference, Christ does not allow that complication to lead to a deconstruction of sex difference itself. She does, however, utilize the image of a continuum in all gender and sexuality issues, other than biological sex. Thus, while masculinity and femininity, and heterosexuality and homosexuality are still, as concepts, set in opposition to one another, Christ now recognizes positions in between the poles, although she does not specify what these positions are nor what their significance might be.

Another important consideration which Christ does not address in "Why Women Need the Goddess" is that of racial categories. Her use of Ntosake Shange's play, "for colored girls who have considered suicide/when the rainbow is enuf," where "a tall beautiful black woman rises from despair to cry out, 'I found God in myself and I loved her fiercely'" (1979: 273), is somewhat problematic. She uses this image to represent all women. Yet, as Himani Bannerji argues:

> Feminist essentialism [such as Christ proposes], with its hypothetical/ synthetic woman subject, cannot situate women in history and society. As such, it eradicates real contradictions among women themselves and creates a myth ("woman") and an abstraction, by isolating gender from all other social relations. (1995: 68)

For Christ, there is no querying into the differing implications of finding God within oneself for a black woman or a white woman in the context of American colonialism and racism. She does not address differing power relations, differing social constructions of black womanhood and white womanhood, differing religious heritages. Instead, she implies that there is such a thing as a universal female religious experience.

In *Rebirth of the Goddess* Christ moves to a recognition that her thealogy cannot be universal or definitive. She realizes that her concepts of the Goddess are influenced by her geography, sexuality, nationality, race, and so on. Thus my concerns about the lack of race analysis in "Why Women Need the Goddess" are addressed to some extent in this later work. Here she once again talks of the Ntosake Shange play. But instead of equating the black woman character's experience as potentially representative of all women, she recognizes, in particular, the significance of unsettling the racialization of God along with gender/sex. In finding God within herself, God not only becomes a woman (a challenge to the patriarchal "male" God) but God also becomes black (a challenge to the white supremacy of western patriarchy) (1997, 95).[6] This inclusion of the beginnings of analysis of race makes Christ's project more clear and more specific. She is clearly speaking from her own location and calling for a dialogue with women in other locations. She is moving away from "woman" as a unifying subject to a recognition of differences among women's experiences. However, *Rebirth of the Goddess* certainly does not address all of the issues raised in my reading of "Why Women Need the Goddess." Christ has not yet moved to question the category of "female" as a construction. Nor has she found a way to talk about women and the Goddess without reducing the "essence" of women to reproduction. She does, however, begin to recognize the influences of racialization on women's experiences and lived realities.

I strongly believe that for Christ's thealogy to do the work she wants it to do—deconstructing patriarchal religion, and reintegrating that which has been separated by patriarchal dualisms, in order to empower women in their everyday lives—"woman" and "female" as conceptual categories must be further unsettled. I am not arguing for the outright rejection of "woman" or "female" as categories. As Butler writes:

> To call a presupposition into question is not the same as doing away with it; rather, it is to free it from its metaphysical lodgings in order to understand what political interests were secured in and by that metaphysical placing, and thereby to permit the term to occupy and to serve very different political aims. [...] This unsettling of "matter" can be understood as initiating new possibilities, new ways for bodies to matter. (1993: 30)

"Woman" and "female" are social realities if not necessarily biological givens. However, it is important to understand how they are being used and continually constructed and how they relate to other racial and sexual identities. Further unsettling must involve a rethinking of the symbolism of the Goddess and what a female deity might mean to feminist theories which question the dualistic male-female construction of sex. Rethinking Goddess imagery in this context brings more questions than it does answers. Does Goddess imagery necessarily reinforce the male-female dichotomy or can it provide a balancing corrective to patriarchal religious symbolism? Can Goddess symbolism produce a cultural/religious shift to a point where a sexually ambiguous deity is conceivable? Or, will it continue to reinforce a definition of women as unitary and in binary opposition to men? These questions do not negate the important work Christ has done in Goddess thealogy. They allow other feminist thealogians and religious studies scholars to build on her work to move into the future— shaping and moulding what is useful, taking down what needs to be "unbuilt." The future is before us. These questions I have raised, which come out of a re-examination of Carol Christ's reflections, can help carve some paths into the new millennium of feminist religious creation.

[1]There is not room in the confines of this essay to discuss in detail the significance of ritual magic in contemporary Goddess spirituality. Very simply it involves a belief in energy forces which can be shaped through willpower to achieve concrete results. See Starhawk, *Dreaming the Dark: Magic, Sex and Politics* (1982) for a more detailed account.

[2]It is unclear how Christ is using the term "sexual identity." It seems that she is referring to a combination of sex and gender (embodied femininity maybe?). But what about sexuality and sexual orientation?

[3]It seems unlikely that patriarchal religious symbolism allows homosexual men, or men who are transvestites or transsexuals, to have their "full sexual identity affirmed as being in the image and likeness of God."

[4]It is significant that many Goddess worshippers are involved in ecofeminism, although not all ecofeminists would maintain the "naturalness" of women's connection to the earth outside of patriarchal constructions. See Irene Diamond and Gloria Feman Orenstein's *Reweaving the World: The Emergence of Ecofeminism* (1990) for a variety of stances on this issue.

[5]Christ does recognize these latter relationships as included in women's bonds but she does not indicate how Goddess symbolism relates to them or affirms them.

[6]See Christ's *Diving Deep and Surfacing: Women Writers on Spiritual Quest* (1980) for an expanded discussion of Ntosake Shange.

References

Bannerji, Himani. *Thinking Through: Essays on Feminism, Marxism, and Anti-Racism.* Toronto: Women's Press, 1995.

Butler, Judith. *Bodies that Matter.* New York: Routledge, 1993.

Christ, Carol P. "Why Women Need the Goddess: Phenomenological, Psychological and Political Reflections." *Womanspirit Rising: A Feminist Reader in Religion.* Eds. Carol P. Christ and Judith Plaskow. New York: Harper and Row, Publishers, 1979.

Christ, Carol P. *Diving Deep and Surfacing: Woman Writers on Spiritual Quest.* Boston: Beacon Press, 1980.

Christ, Carol P. *Rebirth of the Goddess: Finding Meaning in Feminist Spirituality.* Reading, Massachusetts: Addison-Wesley Publishing Company, Inc., 1997.

Diamond, Irene and Gloria Feman Orenstein, eds. *Reweaving the World: The Emergence of Ecofeminism.* San Francisco: Sierra Books, 1990.

Gross, Rita M. *Feminism and Religion.* Boston: Beacon Press, 1996.

Grosz, Elizabeth. *Volatile Bodies: Toward a Corporeal Feminism.* Bloomington and Indianapolis: Indiana University Press, 1994.

Kessler, Suzanne and Wendy McKenna. *Gender:An Ethnomethodological Approach.* Chicago: University of Chicago Press, 1978.

Starhawk. *Dreaming the Dark: Magic, Sex and Politics.* Boston: Beacon Press, 1982.

Talking About Violence Against Women

Deconstructing Uncontested Discourses

Debra Langan

Violence against women is a topic that has received considerable research attention, particularly during the last two decades of the twentieth century. In response to this literature, there has been an increased awareness of, and attempts to deal with, interpersonal and systemic violence within the universities. Security measures within universities have been increased. Sexual harassment policies have been developed, and complaint centres and race and ethnic relations offices have been established. Education now includes informing the university community about harassment issues. Gender equity committees and policies have been instituted. Notwithstanding these and other developments, as we move into the new millennium, violence against women on campus persists in many forms. New insights and actions are essential to eradicate violence on (and off) campus.

Through deconstructing how talk in social interaction contributes to the perpetuation of ideologies around gendered power relations, my research breaks new ground in terms of its approach to the social problem of violence against women. The findings show that interpersonal discussions about violence against women continue to be characterized by dominant discourses which, for the most part, are not successfully contested in small group discussions. My research is on the edge, I would argue, when compared to the bulk of the work that has been done on violence against women (the *epistemological* edge) and in terms of its potential for insights that can further social and political action (the *cutting* edge).

Drawing on recent feminist theorizing in social psychology, in this analysis violence against women is conceptualized as a manifestation of gendered power relations, an historical expression of male domination manifested within the family and currently reinforced by the institutions, economic arrangements, and sexist division of labour within capitalist society (Schechter 1991: 209). My focus is on an understanding of social relations at a micro-, social psychological level by considering how interpersonal interactions are structured by macro-level phenomena such as discourse and ideologies. The research is modelled after research that looks to postmodern literary theory and discourse analysis as a way in which to study gender and/or subjectivity (e.g. Henriques 1984; Wetherell 1986; Rossiter 1988; Gavey 1989; Unger 1990; Lather 1991). Also influential is the research that focuses on the reproduction of ideologies through discourse (e.g., Fowler 1979; Said 1979; Trew 1979; Potter *et al.* 1984; Potter and Wetherell 1987; Wetherell *et al.* 1987; Billig 1988; Hodge and Kress 1988; Gough 1998; Edley and Wetherell, 1999). Finally, those who have attempted to apply both postmodern theory and discourse analysis (in some cases, to an understanding of gender and subjectivity) *within the group context* have offered important ground for thought (e.g. Kress and Fowler 1979; Fairclough 1989; Hollway 1989; Edwards and Potter 1992; Lovering 1995).

Guided by the postmodern literature, I came to question how gendered power relations get reproduced and/or challenged through discursive productions, or talk. Using the Small Groups Laboratory at York University, I involved undergraduate students in small group discussions which centered on forms of violence against women on campus—"chilly climate" (an uncomfortable, or hostile, environment), sexual harassment, and sexual assault. In the first phase of this research (1993), twelve groups were assembled—seven groups of women and five groups of men.[1] In both the women's and men's groups, I or my male colleague[2] (respectively) encouraged participants to elaborate on their understandings of these topics, and we also challenged them to explore dominant discourses and contradictions in talk.

In the analysis that follows, I begin by highlighting the ideological content of individuals' discursive productions.[3] Secondly, I analyze the links between individuals' investments in discourses and small group processes, because interactions represent an important social context that has largely been ignored in discourse analyses. Thirdly, I consider how liberal discourses are constructed so that they successfully function to perpetuate dominant ideologies.

Ideological Content

"Dominant discourses" are those that were deemed to support the status quo, and because these seem commonsensically 'true' to those who professed them, they are particularly powerful. As Gavey notes: "[Dominant] discourses, which support and perpetuate existing power relations, tend to constitute the subjectivity of most of the people most of the time" (1989: 464). Although I had anticipated that my sample of students would be more invested in critical discourses that challenge existing social arrangements (given what I believed to be their exposure to critical analyses within the university), the marginality and absence of participants' positioning in critical discourses was a notable finding. Furthermore, both the women's and men's groups were similarly invested in dominant discourses.

In all of the groups, the liberal ideology of individualism was frequently expressed through discourse that represents social problems as produced by individuals (Rossiter 1988: 147), such that the broader social and ideological processes are ignored (Potter *et al.* 1984: 61). From this perspective, an individual is often presented as possessing the power to control whether or not violence is experienced, hence it is at the level of the individual that change is conceptualized. For example, during a discussion of "chilly climate," this participant's talk focussed on the personal control that she has over her experience. The repeated use of the pronoun "I" in this excerpt signals her positioning within a "personal power" discourse:

> *I think I want to speak when I want to speak, I know that women do have some disadvantages over men, but myself personally, if I know I'm at a disadvantage, I'll make the best to be at an advantage. I don't, I don't listen to that. I have a mind of my own, and if I find I'm at fault, I'm at fault, if I can do anything to benefit myself over what a man can possibly get, I mean I'm strong-willed, I don't believe in that. I don't know if that's from upbringing or anything, but my parents always told me, "You can be whatever you want to be, and no man is better than you." (Alida)*

This quote illustrates how a personal power discourse is closely tied to meritocracy discourse. The idea is that if an individual puts his or her mind to it, and works hard, s/he will achieve whatever goal is sought. Again, it is the individual who is seen to be in control of the social situation. For example, the participant indicates that her successes or failures are due to her efforts alone.

Debra Langan

This view runs contrary to an understanding of individual achievement as attributable, to a large extent, to social conditions.

The ideology of individualism was also contextualized through talk that attributes chilly climate to psychological factors. For example, this participant commented on feeling alienated in lecture when her science professor said that "women are stupid":

> ... (T)hat was just the ... [professor's] personality ... professor-wise they were just ignorant, it wasn't to do with the gender issue I don't think. (Sabrina)

Here, the individual professor's personality is cited as the problem, even though during the discussion, a number of similar examples served to illustrate the ways in which this view of women is shared and perpetuated by various lecturers.

Rooted in the ideology of individualism is the ideology of equality, and this was a prevalent theme in the groups. To illustrate: The assumption behind meritocracy discourse (which conveys the ideology of individualism) is that both men and women have *equal* opportunities to succeed in the world, such that the outcome rests on their *individual* efforts to succeed. These notions of equality work to conceal *actual* social relations of inequality between men and women (and racial groups, and social classes, and age groups, etc.). The next excerpt is typical of how participants argued that men and women experience chilly climate to the same extent: "I think it goes both ways basically ... you cannot say a chilly climate towards one gender and not towards the other" (Pamela).

Our probes about chilly climate were often met with silence until a probe similar to the following was put forth:

> Some feel that it is feminists on campus who make a big deal about women feeling less comfortable on campus, when, actually, both men and women, regardless of racial background feel the same on campus. What is your view on this? (Langan 1997: 183)

Overwhelmingly, this probe led to discussions similar to the following:

> Gina: *Often times I feel uncomfortable because of the people at the university, not to offend any feminists here, who are real feminists, and who*

make such a big deal out of it. And I take the flack for it … .with all of the sexual harassment, that's a real problem, and I realize that, but sometimes it's taken too far. A lot of people look, a lot of men on campus look at the instances that have gone too far. They look at women as all being like that, as all looking at everything going too far…. I can't think of a specific example, but there's some, some feminists that you know, like one, a man or something will say one slightly maybe, maybe slightly sexist comment, and they blow it totally out of proportion and try to get the guy fired, and try and dig into his past and destroy his career and that happens, maybe not so much at York….

Leanne: *I think there are situations, I had, one of my classes in first year, one of the guys was doing a woman's study course … and he had a female professor that was a very radical feminist, and he felt that he was getting kind of, the reverse extreme of that, that he was getting a bad experience. And from what he was describing to me, and I believed him, he was getting a prejudiced, a reversed prejudice….*

Gina: *I've had a lot of men that treat me badly because I'm a woman on a feminist campus…. And they look down on me because of that, and I'm not a feminist. And I don't want to be looked at as one.*

This excerpt illustrates the way in which feminists are blamed for fabricating a chilly climate problem.

When sexual harassment was the topic, discussions centred on difficulties around defining sexual harassment. Some narrowly defined what constitutes an instance of sexual harassment, often stipulating that inappropriate touching (at the very minimum) must have occurred:

I have my own definition of sexual harassment … .I consider [that] when someone touches me in the wrong places, I call that sexual harassment. (Alida)

When you get into the actual like physical stage of like touching and things … then adjust the problem. But I mean, things are going to go overboard when they keep breaking things down. (Keri)

Here there is a failure to acknowledge that sexually harassing behaviours occur also through verbal and non-verbal interactions.

Those who advocated a narrow definition argued that broader definitions distract attention away from "real" instances of sexual harassment. In the following excerpt, Evi argues that a broad definition allows for a debate about what constitutes sexual harassment, and as a result fuels a position that minimizes sexual harassment.

> ... *I think a lot of times when ... [sexual harassment is] actually real, it's not going to receive the attention it deserves because then everything's going to be sexual harassment. So when it really is ... .it's going to be just dismissed, "Oh yea, you know, you were drunk, blah, blah, blah...."* (Evi)

Similarly, Shannon opposes a broad definition of sexual harassment:

> *[Feminists] ... probably shouldn't be defining what sexual harassment is. They shouldn't be saying that it includes sitting too close together, and you know, that's what it seems to be. It's gone from making someone feel uncomfortable, or, I don't know where it started, sexual advances, and now it's including, well you name it. You take any situation and you can manipulate it to think someone's harassing you.* (Shannon)

This latter quote illustrates the way in which the "feminists have gone too far" theme discussed earlier was often embodied in criticisms of broad definitions:

Contrary to those who advocate narrow definitions, some participants rendered a definition so vague that sexual harassment becomes virtually unidentifiable. For these participants, a definition can only be individualistic because personal perceptions differ as to what sexual harassment is. For example:

> Walter: *I don't know, I think the criteria is so much, like you can't define it. You cannot possibly define it because what a woman might think a man is doing, as far as like a gaze, something like a gaze, it might be innocent, and it might not be innocent. How can you possibly define that? How can someone file a complaint, say with the police, and say "This man was gazing at me improperly." And what's he supposed to come back and say? "No I wasn't." ... [H]ow can you define the line where it's right and it's wrong? It's not possible, something like that.*

Nick: *Everybody's got their own scale.*

Such talk dismisses the existence, or the possibility, of a standardized definition and code of conduct for all individuals. The impression gained is that if you can't define sexual harassment, it exists only in the minds of some.

Improved communication between individual men and women was frequently posited as the way in which to deal with the dilemma of defining sexual harassment:

> ... *[I]t all boils down to communication. If you say what you're going to do, and you do what you're going to say. You know, I mean, that's what it basically boils down to: People aren't communicating. If a guy takes a woman's behaviour wrongly, you know, it takes two to tango, it's both their fault because they're both not talking.* (Peter)

Again, this discourse negates the social, political, and ideological nature of sexual harassment, and reduces it to an isolated problem that exists between individuals.

As with chilly climate talk, individualistic ideologies were joined with ideologies of equality when sexual harassment was the topic. To demonstrate that men's experience is equal to women's, talk turned to stories about cases where men have been victims of sexual harassment and sexual assault. The result is that the equality theme led to a characterization of men as the most victimized. While both women's and men's groups incorporated this discursive theme of "guys-are-victims-too," the content and function of the discourse generally differed between women's and men's groups. In the women's groups, the guys-are-victims-too talk arose in response to critical questions or comments which suggested that it is overwhelmingly *women* who are typically the victims of violence. In response, the point was stressed that both women *and* men are subject to violence:

> *It's not chilly just for females. I know some males too who would find it chilly ... so it's not just a feminist thing.* (Kyla)

> *A friend of mine was attacked right outside, a man, right outside the doors.... So, it goes both ways, I think....* (Tanya)

When the male groups talked about how guys-are-victims-too, men's victimization was not characterized as being the same (i.e., circumstantially) as women's victimization. Instead, men were represented as the victims *of* women, in that women were blamed for the rise in critical talk which challenges men's positions of power within the society. Most of the men focussed on themselves as persecuted, not only by *feminists*, but also by *women* in general. In addition to explicit references that characterized women as men's enemy, in the men's groups, the misogynist talk implicitly blamed the critiques that challenge gendered power relationships. The following comment portrays men as victims of the current critical climate:

> ... [J]ust to be safe yourself, as a male in this climate, you have to ensure that there's no way you can get yourself in danger. If you're seen following a woman, and a police officer stops you, the police state-class-climate if you want to call it that is you're guilty until proven innocent no matter what it is, sexual harassment, sexual assault, it's almost like you're in Mexico or another state where it's guilt, guilty until proven innocent instead of innocent until proven guilty.... (Vince)

This produces the impression that critical, or counter, ideologies are in fact dominant ideologies. The result is that the men's group discussions portray men as being the 'real' victims, the members of society who are marginal and subject to women's power. The men's groups' guys-are-victims-too message works to divert attention away from the argument that women are overwhelmingly the victims of violence on university campuses. The focus instead is shifted to men who are cast as victims of counter ideologies and critical talk which seeks to challenge men's power within society. Women in general are blamed for the proliferation of critical discourses. As was mentioned earlier, the majority of the women disavowed an association with feminism and feminists because feminists "gave women a bad name." The men-as-persecuted theme in the male group discussions suggests that formalized feminism has, in fact, given women "a bad name." Even though relatively few women are invested in feminist positions, women in general are blamed for the (alleged) impact of feminist discourse.

The majority of the discussions around sexual assault contained patriarchal ideologies—beliefs about gender relations which reinforce and maintain the authoritative positioning of men, and the oppressive situations of women. Patriarchal ideologies naturalize social processes—that is, it is taken for granted that incidents that qualify as social events are, instead, inevitable

events of nature. The theme of "violence is natural" is supported by participants' essentialist descriptions which took the form of definitive statements
either about what "girls are" or "guys are." Hare-Mustin and Marecek point to
the way in which biological sexual differences are typically viewed as synony-
mous with gender differences:

> ... [There is a] pervasive cultural belief that we have not created
> gender, but that gender is natural and largely explained by the
> biological differences of males and females. When we associate
> gender merely with sexual differences, gender itself becomes con-
> strued as difference, and gender differences are therefore also seen as
> natural. (1990: 188)

The following example from the data illustrates this notion of biological
pre-determination:

> *I think [sexual assault] is part of a larger problem ... especially ... if you look
> at it biologically: men's hormones fluctuate daily, their testosterone levels
> rise and fall all day. Women fluctuate monthly, so I mean, come on. That's
> got to tell you something right there. And I mean the statistics on how many
> times men think about sex daily as opposed to how many times women think
> of it.* (Emylene)

The participants' views of sexual assault espoused patriarchal ideology,
specifically "paternalism," "a concept of power which combines the element
of benevolence with the elements of dominance and subordination" (Davis *et
al.* 1991: 23). Paternalism involves both a relationship of asymmetry *and* a
relationship wherein the person in authority restricts and coerces the freedom
of another for that other's own good (Davis *et al.* 1991: 23). In the discussions,
men are repeatedly described as taking care of women in a way that renders
women "the weaker sex." The aforementioned ideological themes of natural-
ism and biological determinism reinforce paternalism—because men are seen
as naturally stronger than women, they should therefore protect women. In
almost every group, it was noted that the women could call on some of the guys
they knew to escort them from one place to another on campus, typically after
dark.

> *... [T]here would be a group of guys each night who were free, and if you*

had to walk somewhere you'd call them and they would walk you. We'd have our own security within our building. And they're people you'd know, and people you'd trust. (Tanya)

In this example, the asymmetrical nature of the relationship between the women and the men is clear—the women's freedom is restricted by the availability and willingness of the men to come and escort them. Although they have benevolent intentions, the men are in a position of power.

Commensurate with this guys-as-protectors theme was talk about security measures which also proceeds from the assumption that violence is a naturally-occurring phenomenon within our society. Security measures are (naturally) in place to combat violence. While both the women's and men's groups produced examples of the guys-as-protectors theme, the security talk was evidenced primarily among the women—they viewed security measures as holding the promise of a solution to violence. These security measures included both formal security guard surveillance as well as individual strategies such as scheduling classes during the daytime, walking with keys ready to scratch an assailant's face, and walking with others to one's car. The women tended to talk about *how* to be secure as if knowing how to do this solves the problem of being at risk as a woman. Security talk reflects paternalism in that security measures are indicative of a power imbalance wherein the freedom of women is curtailed and the power of those in authority is bolstered.

"Fear of sexual assault" was another prevalent theme within the women's groups. The following excerpt is one example:

Tanya: ... *[Rape] would be the worst thing that could ever happen to me. I think and it sounds really extreme and really bad and everything. But I feel that if, not necessarily with date rape or something, but if a gentleman had, I shouldn't call him a gentleman, if a guy had a gun to my head and he's going to rape me, I'm sorry, I'd rather be shot, like it's just so... it's just something that's so personal, and I don't think that I could live through it.*

Alida: *You give me the goosebumps.*

Tanya: *I'm sorry. But I think, it's just, it's just a personal issue. It has nothing to do with, you know, with any of the feminism or the, you know, the campus or anything.*

This discourse is best understood within the context of the guys-as-protectors and the security talk. The paternalistic nature of "fear" talk explains why I held contradictory feelings during these segments of the discussions. I felt sympathetic towards the women when they talked about how the fear of sexual assault frightened them. I also felt humiliated because of the way in which they perpetuated their status as victims through the fear of sexual assault discourse (the tone of the discussion is one of helpless surrender); the guys-as-protectors discourse; and the security discourse.

A theme of individualism also recurred during discussions of sexual assault. In the following example, Marianne expressed her determination to deal with the threat of violence:

> ... I take karate, and like I have alarms, like everything in my bag. Because I'm not going to stop my life 'cause of this kind of stuff, because if I have to take a class from 6:00 to 9:00, because that's the only time I can take the class, then I'm going to take the class.... I rely on myself ... I feel like, why should I have to do that? That's not fair to me.... You do have to take it on yourself.

The woman is also seen as responsible for sexual assault when it happens. This "blame the victim" theme was manifest in a number of ways. At times, participants pointed to communication problems as contributing to sexual assault, the woman being the one who is unclear about her wishes around sexual activity:

Bruce: *Well, if women want to have sex, be honest about it, don't be cóy.*

Vince: *If ... [women are] going to use the word "No," mean it, because too many guys hear "No," and think "Okay, try harder...."*

Scott: *I guess women don't want to be classed as easy.*

Vince: *Exactly. A woman has to play the game because if she's not, she's considered a tramp or whatever.*

Scott: *Or a slut...*

Vince: *So the women play ... that little game, so a lot of guys, unfortu-*

nately, when they hear that little word, "No," still have this, "Okay, she's playing coy with me." And I'm sure that in a lot of cases that no is a real "No," but they continue anyways because they're so used to the coy "No."

Bruce: *Well the problem too is that they say no, to be coy, and the guy, "Okay ... " and you keep on making out, and eventually they don't say anything when you try the second time, and that's consent, or is it? The problem comes when she said no at the beginning of the night when you tried to grap her tit, and then she didn't say a word when you were pulling off her panties and going down on her, except to moan a lot, and is that date rape? Is that date rape?*

On other occasions, women are portrayed as "asking for it" (i.e., sexual assault) because of flirtatious signs that are communicated through behaviour or appearance:

Santina: *... [Y]ou're always going to have those women who are there, like, they're going to tease, and especially you know, there's a problem on like, pub night sort of stuff like that when everyone's drinking, and a lot of the girls they do lead the guys on, and they flirt around, and stuff, and I'm not saying*

Rachel: *But if they're drunk they won't be aware of what they're doing.*

Santina: *I'm not saying they're asking for it like,*

Rachel: *Yea, no one is asking for it,*

Santina: *Just because they're flirting, but, but sometimes they do let things happen*

Kyla: *They're putting themselves in a vulnerable situation.*

Typical in discussions like this is the use of a disclaimer which notes that the victims are not to blame, followed by talk which then blames the victim, a construction which works to legitimize dominant discourse.

Talk about sexual assault provides a good example of how various discursive themes are interconnected in discussions and work to perpetuate dominant ideologies. As already noted, the view that violence is natural provides the foundation for guys-as-protectors talk and fear talk, these in turn supporting an acceptance of security measures as necessary. These themes are all rooted in ideologies of individualism and paternalism: the onus is on the individual to take care of herself, through a variety of security precautions which benevolently exist to calm her fears and to help her. The participants' concern with security overrides more critical themes (if they even get introduced), and the women talk about security strategies with great enthusiasm. It is these kinds of interrelationships among discourses and ideologies and participants' investments in them that make them so difficult to contest successfully, or to deconstruct.

Further complicating matters is the way in which discourses are not characterized by unitary or consistent themes, but are instead made-up of themes that are frequently in opposition. Often critical comments were embedded in what was for the most part dominant discourse. That is, it was more typical for participants to make 'the odd' critical comment during what was otherwise dominant discourse. In the following excerpt, the participant deliberates about whether or not a particular type of woman is targeted for a violent attack:

> ... *If I was the type of person that wanted to come after somebody, what type of person would I come after? So I'm not going to be that type of person. Like you know how they have, like there's no set hard and fast rules about only certain types of girls get attacked. But, there are certain type girls, if, you're not prepared, you have more chances of being attacked.* (Marianne)

Initially, this participant suggests that there is a particular type of person who gets attacked in that she says: "I'm not going to be that type of person." Here she individualizes the problem of violence, and places responsibility on the victim to prevent violence by being a particular type of individual. In the next sentence, she states that there are *not* particular types who get attacked: "there's no set hard and fast rules about only certain types of girls who get attacked" thus removing the responsibility from the victim. In the subsequent sentence she returns to her earlier positioning within an ideology of individualism by acknowledging that: "there are certain type girls, if, you're not prepared, you have more chances of being attacked." These kinds of contradictions are evident throughout the group discussions.

Debra Langan

Investments in Discourse and Group Process

To this point I have been talking about the groups as a collection of individuals; my focus now shifts to a discussion of the group discourse overall. The interactional context of a group of individuals calls into question how the dynamics of the group relate to the content of the talk. Since discourse analyses are premised on the belief that people produce particular kinds of talk according to the situation (i.e., there is no one true state of affairs awaiting discovery through research), the value of a group analysis lies not in the increased validity of the data. Rather, the group is interesting because it is the usual venue for talk, and, in group settings, participants have the potential to influence one another's talk. While experiences pre-exist language, a description of them does not. I believe that many of the participants have experienced, in some way, situations on campus that I would describe as instances of chilly climate, sexual harassment, and even sexual assault. This is the position of Kelly who maintains that in their lifetime, most women experience some form of "sexual violence" a general term which covers all forms of abuse, coercion or force from men (1987: 46, 59). It could be that the majority of these women and men did not have access to, and are therefore not familiar with, more critical bodies of thought on the topics presented. It could also be that they chose not to position themselves critically in talk. As Gavey notes, "systems of meaning such as feminism are currently limited in their power because they are marginalized and unavailable yet as subject positions ... ." (1989: 464). If it is the case that some of the participants have been exposed to, but show little or no investment in, critical discourses, then the question arises as to why this is the case.

A consideration of group process offers some answers to these questions. First, there is a tendency for group participants to exhibit a high degree of consensus (Gilbert and Mulkay 1984: 189) on topics early in discussions. Because liberal and patriarchal ideologies dominated the discursive productions of these groups, it follows that a movement toward a consensus would discourage critical talk. In the majority of the groups, there was one participant whose talk was largely critical in nature, but who still indicated some affiliation with dominant ideologies. At times, this "lone critic" wavered in his/her critical position, such that s/he came to express a mixture of critical and dominant views. In other instances, the lone critic withdrew from the discussion altogether, typically during the first half of the discussion.

Secondly, as is clear from my study, the supposed normalcy of the dominant discourses in these groups makes anyone who challenges them risk being stigmatized as deviant, this working to silence critical talk. For example it could be that most of the women in this study avoided identification as a victim of sexual harassment because of the stigmatized status of being a victim. Kitzinger and Thomas discuss how women choose to adopt the label of victim according to whether it would be in their best interests to do so in the situation. They state:

> The term "sexual harassment" describes female subordination. When women say, to themselves or to other people, "I am *not* being sexually harassed," one of the things they are saying is, "I am *not* a victim. I am not a subordinated person." (1995: 35)

For similar reasons, the women in the groups were unlikely to identify as feminists because of the anti-feminist sentiments which are perpetuated in dominant discourses. The men, because they tend to be targeted in critical discourses on gender, avoided talk that might lead to their being stigmatized either as perpetrators of violence, or as discussed earlier, supporters of feminist ideologies. Hence, the avoidance of stigma may explain, in part, participants' reluctance to invest in critical positions within the groups. Understanding that participants tried to avoid stigma also helps to explain the scarcity of talk about dimensions of difference other than gender; when the topic of racial difference was raised, for example, frequently the ideology of equality was espoused. As discussed previously, the difficulty in publicly positioning oneself in critical discourse stems from a fear of being stigmatized as "one of those" who is deviant from the norm (e.g., black, lower class, homosexual, older, physically or mentally challenged, etc.) and (unjustifiably) defiant. Regardless of whether the differentiating feature of identity is apparent, the oppressed also experience fluctuating investments in critical discourse (Young and Majury 1995: 352), and they fear being labelled "a troublemaker."

Thirdly, the participants who espoused critical discourse (typically one per group) did so at great length, in a way that suggested they saw themselves as "experts" on the topics of discussion. The presence of "an expert" appeared to annoy the other participants, and "the functioning of the group as a whole can easily be disrupted by friendship pairs, 'experts,' or uncooperative participants" (Morgan 1993: 44). Regardless of the investments of the others in the group, the expert's participation served to alienate others in the group such that an 'us against the expert' alliance formed among group participants. The

Debra Langan

result is that those 'other' participants became united around dominant ideologies seemingly in opposition to the expert, perhaps more so than might otherwise have been the case.

Constructions of Liberal Discourse

A microscopic analysis of how talk is constructed serves to shed light on how liberal discourses successfully marginalize critical discourses within small group interactions. As was noted earlier, the following excerpt illustrated the dominant discourse around how the problem of chilly climate has been created by feminists:

> *I can't think of a specific example, but there's some, some feminists that you know, like one, a man or something will say one slightly maybe, maybe slightly sexist comment, and they blow it totally out of proportion and try to get the guy fired, and try and dig into his past and destroy his career and that happens, maybe not so much at York....* (Gina)

Linguistic structures that incorporate conditional statements and contrast statements are very effective in producing convincing arguments for an audience (Potter and Wetherell 1987: 47). In this excerpt, the use of conditional statement structures is evidenced by an "if this," "then that" construction. This technique can be highlighted by rearranging the discourse as follows:

> A1: If [a man ... will say one ... slightly sexist comment]
> A2: then [(some feminists) will blow it totally out of proportion and try to get the guy fired ... and destroy his career]

Another persuasive aspect of the above-noted extract is what Pomerantz has called the "extreme case" formulation (Potter and Wetherell 1987: 47). By using extremes, a more convincing argument is made. In this excerpt, a number of extreme statements strengthen an anti-feminist argument: a man only has to say *one* comment (the lowest possible number); this comment has only to be *slightly* sexist (as opposed to sexist); the result is that it will be blown *totally* out of proportion ("out of proportion" is an extreme phrase on its own, but with "totally" as a modifier, its extreme quality is magnified); the end result will be *firing* (the most extreme formal reprimand possible in the workplace) and a

| 102

destroyed career (the man will *never* be able to work again in his chosen career). And finally, in this example, disclaimers serve to "ward off" statements which could be offensive (Hewitt and Stokes qtd. in Potter and Wetherell 1987: 48) and which could result in embarrassment for the speaker. "*I can't think of a specific example*" is a disclaimer which allows the speaker to construct a hypothetical scenario which cannot be factually verified. This allows for the use of extreme case formulations which may, in reality, not be the case (or very rarely be the case). The comment, "*maybe not so much at York*" similarly functions to remove the scenario from the context with which all those present, presumably, are most familiar. Therefore, it is more difficult to dispute the claims that are made if scenarios like this are occurring at universities other than York. Furthermore, this disclaimer serves to "ward off" any offense which might be experienced by one or more feminists that might be present in the group.

Concluding

My research addresses several gaps in the literature on violence against women. First, the study links macro- and micro-level analyses: it examines how macro-level ideologies and discourses work together through micro-level interactions, to help sustain violence against women. Secondly, most of the previous research on sexual assault and sexual harassment has addressed "what" questions, like: What is the prevalence of sexual assault? What definitions of sexual assault/harassment are employed by students? What factors are correlated with incidents of violence? This study raises new "what" questions: What discourses are most/least prevalent in the group discussions? What ideological themes are embodied in these discourses? Thirdly, in focusing on what students, *in the presence of others*, have to say about chilly climate, sexual harassment, and sexual assault, the analysis attends to the dynamic processes of discursive work through which discourses are reproduced/challenged. Attention to this context raises new "how" questions: How do the micro-level processes within the group operate to perpetuate and/or challenge discourses? How is talk constructed by the individual? How is talk constructed by the group? How does talk work to achieve particular effects within the group? And lastly, and perhaps most importantly, this research is politically motivated; discourses are seen as having social consequences which the research process must work to change. That is, its purpose is not to investigate whether, or to what extent women are victimized, rather it is grounded in the assertion that women and other minority groups routinely experience violence on (and off) campus, a reality which necessitates a "passionately interested inquiry" (Gill 1995: 169). By unraveling the ways in which talk works to perpetuate the taken-for-granted realities about gender relations—and, therefore, gender violence—we move closer to dealing with the question: How can dominant discourses be more successfully challenged, and alternative, critical ideologies effectively promoted? This line of inquiry, in combination with other measures, holds promise for us as we continue to work toward affecting changes in social relations, and in particular, social relations of power which perpetuate and reinforce male violence against women.

[1]My data collection began in 1993 for the purpose of completing my doctoral dissertation. For the past two years (1999-2001), I have continued to gather and analyze data through similar discourse analysis labs, this being one component of the third-year course that I teach in the Department of Sociology, York University: "Classic and Contemporary Issues in Social Psychology." The more recent data and analysis are in keeping with what I found in the initial phase of the research.

[2]Karl Henriques, a Ph.D. student in the Department of Sociology at York University, moderated the groups of men.

[3]The examples that I use for this paper are drawn from the 1993 phase of the research. I have changed the participants' names to ensure confidentiality.

References

Billig, Michael. *Ideological Dilemmas*. London: Sage Publications, 1988.

Davis, Kathy, Monique Leijenaar, and Jantine Oldersma. *The Gender of Power*. London: Sage Publications, 1991.

Edley, Nigel and Margaret Wetherell. "Imagined Futures: Young Men's Talk About Fatherhood and Domestic Life." *British Journal of Social Psychology* 38 (2) (1999): 181-194.

Edwards, Derek and Jonathon Potter. *Discursive Psychology*. London: Sage Publications, 1992.

Fairclough, Norman. *Discourse Analysis*. Cambridge: Polity Press, 1989.

Fowler, Roger. *Language and Control*. London: Routledge and Kegan Paul , 1979.

Gavey, Nicola. "Feminist Poststructuralism and Discourse Analysis: Contributions to Feminist Psychology." *Psychology of Women Quarterly* 13

(1989):459-475.

Gilbert, G. Nigel and Michael Mulkay. *Opening Pandora's Box*. Cambridge: Cambridge University Press, 1984.

Gill, Rosalind. "Relativism, Reflexivity and Politics: Interrogating Discourse Analysis from a Feminist Perspective." *Feminism and Discourse—Psychological Perspectives*. Eds. Sue Wilkinson and Celia Kitzinger. London: Sage Publications, 1995. 165-186.

Gough, Brendan. "Men and the Discursive Reproduction of Sexism: Repertoires of Difference and Equality." *Feminism and Psychology* 8 (1) (1998): 25-49.

Hare-Mustin, Rachel T. and Jeanne Marecek. "Beyond Difference." *Making a Difference: Psychology and the Construction of Gender*. Eds. R. Hare-Mustin and J. Marecek. New Haven: Yale University Press, 1990. 184-201.

Henriques, J. *Changing the Subject: Psychology, Social Regulation and Subjectivity*. London: Methuen, 1984.

Hodge, Robert and Gunther Kress. *Social Semiotics*. Oxford: Basil Blackwell Ltd., 1988.

Hollway, Wendy. *Subjectivity and Method in Psychology: Gender, Meaning and Science*. London: Sage Publications, 1989

Kelly, Liz. "The Continuum of Sexual Violence." *Women, Violence, and Social Control*. Eds. J. Hammer and M. Maynard. New Jersey: Humanities Press International, Inc., 1987. 46-60.

Kitzinger, Celia and Alison Thomas. "Sexual Harassment: A Discursive Approach." *Feminism and Discourse—Psychological Perspectives*. Eds. Sue Wilkinson and Celia Kitzinger. London: Sage Publications, 1995. 32-48.

Kress, Gunther and Roger Fowler. "Interviews." *Language and Control*. Ed. Roger Fowler. London: Routledge and Keagan Paul, 1979. 63-80.

Langan, Debra. "Reproducing Ideologies in Interaction: Talking About Violence Against Women." Unpublished dissertation. Toronto: York University, 1997.

Lather, Patricia Ann. *Getting Smart: Feminist Research and Pedagogy with/in the Postmodern*. London: Routledge, Chapman and Hall, Inc., 1991.

Lovering, Katherine Matthews. "The Bleeding Body: Adolescents Talk About Menstruation." *Feminism and Discourse: Psychological Perspectives*. Eds. Sue Wilkinson and Celia Kitzinger. London: Sage Publications, 1995. 10-31.

Morgan, David L. *Successful Focus Groups: Advancing the State of the Art*. London: Sage Publications, 1993.

Potter, Jonathon, Peter Stringer, and Margaret Wetherell. *Social Texts and Context: Literature and Social Psychology*. London: Routledge and Kegan Paul, 1984.

Potter, Jonathan and Margaret Wetherell. *Discourse and Social Psychology— Beyond Attitudes and Behaviour*. London: Sage Publications, 1987.

Rossiter, Amy. *From Private to Public: A Feminist Exploration of Early Mothering*. Toronto: The Women's Press, 1988.

Said, Edward W. *Orientalism*. New York: Vintage Books, 1979.

Schechter, Susan. *Women and Male Violence*. Boston: South End Press, 1991.

Trew, Tony. "Theory and Ideology at Work." *Language and Control*. Ed. Roger Fowler. London: Routledge and Kegan Paul, 1979. 94-116.

Unger, Rhoda K. "Imperfect Reflections of Reality." *Making a Difference— Psychology and the Construction of Gender*. Eds. Rachel Hare-Mustin and Jeanne Marecek. New Haven: Yale University Press, 1990. 102-149.

Wetherell, Margaret. "Linguistic Repetories and Linguistic Criticism: New Directions for a Social Psychology of Gender." *Feminist Social Psychology—Developing Theory and Practice*. Ed. Sue Wilkinson. Philadelphia: Open University Press, 1986. 77-95.

Wetherell, Margaret, Hilda Stiven, and Jonathan Potter. "Unequal Egalitarianism: A preliminary Study of Discourses Concerning Gender and Employment Opportunities." *British Journal of Social Psychology* 26 (1) (1987): 59-71.

Young, Claire and Diana Majury. "Lesbian Perspectives." *Breaking Anonymity: The Chilly Climate for Women Faculty*. Eds. The Chilly Collective. Waterloo: Wilfred Laurier University Press, 1995. 345-358.

Birth and Reproduction as Perennial Feminist Issues

The Case of Plato and Mary O'Brien

Joanne H. Wright

As we enter a new millennium, we cannot, as feminists, predict what new issues and challenges will arise and direct our energies. However, we continue to face certain perennial issues which, despite the best feminist efforts and the real gains made, persist and require our attention. One such issue is western culture's response to female reproductive abilities. This response takes the form of a public and philosophical conversation or discourse, and it is this discourse that will be investigated here.

Our culture's discourse about reproduction, while certainly multifaceted and complex, is not derived primarily from women's experiences. Indeed, one might expect that pregnancy and birth are human processes about which women could be considered experts, and that their experiences would comprise an important part of our cultural understanding of reproduction. This is not the case. When birth and reproduction are not forgotten entirely, their incorporation into our public and philosophic discourse occurs in such a way as to minimize, undermine, or distort their significance. Our primary public concern with reproduction has been to control and manage it through medical and legal interventions. What is absent is a cultural conversation that weaves the significance of reproduction into the philosophic fabric of human experience. And certainly, women's own understandings of birth and reproduction should form a crucial part of this fabric.[1]

Mary O'Brien (1981), one of the previous millennium's most important western feminist theorists, tried to address this enormous gap and distortion in our cultural discourse about birth and reproduction. In response to Plato, among others, she suggested that our culture's problematical perceptions of reproduction are rooted in the male experience of alienation from reproduction. In her view, men compensate for their envy of women's reproductive abilities by appropriating the language and power of reproduction for the sphere of politics. While women have a (pro)creative potency as a result of their biology, men are not so lucky. The only way that men can compensate for their biological lack is to distort and appropriate the female experience of creative potency for their own realm. Although O'Brien's appropriation thesis struck a resonant chord in feminism, it is not without its difficulties.

In what follows, I develop the beginnings of a response to Mary O'Brien by examining Plato's dialogue of the *Timaeus*. The *Timaeus*, the dialogue in which Plato elaborates his myth of the origins of the universe, is an important text for feminists to examine because it contains some of the most imaginative passages on birth, reproduction, and gender relations extant in political theory.[2] To be clear, the *Timaeus* is a complex dialogue and it is not Plato's specific intent to theorize reproduction. Rather, he employs the language of reproduction strictly as metaphor for understanding the nature of being and politics. In a sense it is fitting that Plato employs this language in that he is trying to convince us that there is a natural order to politics just as there is a natural order to the cosmos; what better way to demonstrate the link between the two than to use the "natural" language of reproduction. What, then, is the real problem with Plato's *Timaeus* and how does it distort reproductive experience?

In brief, the problems with Plato's *Timaeus* are twofold. The first is that the dialogue resembles the creation story of the Hebrew Bible in that men are created first and women second. Second, in his theorizing on the categories of being, Plato uses a patrogenic reproductive metaphor—that is, a metaphor which posits the male as having the real generative power and the female as little more than a passive receptacle.

Plato proposes that men are born alone on the earth, unaccompanied at first by their female counterparts. These men are given sensations and feelings that must be conquered. Invoking the Platonic ontology of soul before body, the character Timaeus states that if men look after, and are attentive to, the needs and health of the soul, they will return to a "blessed and congenial existence."[3] Alternatively, if men misbehave and take inadequate care of their souls, they will be reborn as women. This unrighteous man "at second birth would pass into a woman," and "if he did not desist from evil he would continually be changed into a brute" (42c). Women are a secondary and, clearly, lesser creation; existence as a woman takes the form of a punishment to intemperate men. Women reside on a scale somewhere between men and brute animals. "Human nature was of two kinds," according to Timaeus, "the superior race was of such and such a character, and would be hereafter called man" (42a). The creator has imagined that there are two "kinds" of human beings, but the male is the original sex, the norm. He not only comes first as a creation but has no need whatsoever for the female.

Male self-sufficiency surfaces here as an ideal: men are self-sufficient in life *and* in reproduction. Men's souls, at least, are created independently of women, of their mothers, and they are able to regenerate themselves independently as well. Plato is not explicit about how they are born, or reborn. He is explicitly suggesting, however, that women are a secondary creation to men. [4]

The primacy of the male of the species is compatible with the second reproductive theme in Plato's *Timaeus*—patrogenesis. Indeed, male generative power forms a recurring theme of the dialogue. For example, a father-God is the "artificer and father" to a tier of lesser gods; and the lesser gods "beget" land and sea creatures, including human beings. These new beings, although mortal, must have a part to them that is immortal and of divine origin. And of that "divine part," the father-God pronounces, "I will myself sow the seed" (41c). The male god is the *creator* of the gods beneath him; he is empowered to *bring them forth*. Similarly, the new race of gods will go on to beget living creatures. Although there are female gods in this second tier, there is no mention of a fertilization process, or of a combining of two types of seed, or of the female's distinct capacity, even where birth itself is concerned. Plato demonstrates here his interest in utilizing a particular view of reproduction and birth common in ancient Greece. [5] His patrogenic sympathies—his reliance on the ideal of masculine self-reproduction—resurface in the story of the receptacle.

The receptacle passage originates with Timaeus announcing the need to create a third class of being in addition to the usual two (48e). The first order of being is that of the Forms, the permanent and unchanging ideas on which the physical world is patterned. These Forms, "apprehended by intelligence and reason," are contrasted with the second category of being, the physical world itself. The physical world, the world of becoming, can only imitate the pattern; it is "generated and visible." Comparing these two realms, Timaeus asks, "What is that which always is and has no becoming, and what is that which is always becoming and never is?" (27d). The third category, Timaeus remarks, is "difficult of explanation and dimly seen"; it is "the receptacle, and in a manner the nurse, of all generation" (49b). This receptacle

> must always be called the same, for, inasmuch as she always receives all things, she never departs from her own nature and never, in any way or at any time, assumes a form like that of any of the things which enter into her; she is the natural recipient of all impressions, and is stirred and informed by them, and appears different from time to time by reason of them. (50b-c)

Timaeus employs a reproductive metaphor to explain this obscure concept of the receptacle. The receiving principle, in which generation takes place, can be likened to a mother; the "source or spring" is the father; and "the intermediate nature" which is in process of generation is the child (50d). The main point he is establishing with this metaphor is the passivity and inertness of the receptacle. To emphasize that the receptacle shall have no form of her own, Timaeus compares her to a liquid that "shall be as inodorous as possible" in order to receive a scent of perfume (50e). Plato seems to contradict himself, for if the receptacle never adheres to the form of that which enters her, how can she change her appearance "by reason of them"?

A truly mysterious and elusive concept, the receptacle is sometimes thought to be space, sometimes matter. To house all that is generated, it must occupy a space. Yet, that which is perpetually to receive, the mother and receptacle of all that is created and visible, "is not to be termed earth or air or fire or water ... but is an invisible and formless being which receives all things and in some mysterious way partakes of the intelligible, and is most incomprehensible" (51b). She partakes of the intelligible, the highest order of being, but is simultaneously apprehended only by a "kind of spurious reason" (52b). She is a fleeting shadow, hardly real, and incomprehensible. Moreover, we can have, according to Timaeus, only a "dreamlike sense" of her as "we are unable to cast off sleep and determine the truth" about this being or space (52c).

For the purposes of this article, we need to consider the significance of Plato's use of patrogenic metaphors. Plato is involved in a myth-creating exercise in the *Timaeus*, so it is unlikely that he entertained patrogensis as a serious scientific theory. Nevertheless, myth is not politically benign, and Plato's choice to depict men as autonomous and self-generating serves a political purpose.

It is tempting to surmise that Plato deliberately uses patrogenesis to further the ideological cause of women's seclusion in ancient Athens. After all, this patrogenic creation story is entertained against the backdrop of a masculinist political configuration, one in which women themselves are almost entirely excluded from participation in many aspects of Athenian public life. But in fact, Plato's use of this metaphor may have more to do with a life that he desires for men, a life of masculine virtue, than with an overt project to subordinate women. Certainly there is a strong relationship between origin stories like the *Timaeus* and birth metaphors—how could this not be the case when an origin story is an attempt to understand where we come from? But it is a complex connection and one that cannot easily be assessed.

I want to return now to Mary O'Brien's appropriation thesis, which suggests that male philosophers and politicians are drawn to origin stories because they are alienated from the material experience of reproduction. Men's reproductive alienation leads them to appropriate women's experiences of pregnancy and birth for the masculine realm of politics. According to this appropriation theory, male philosophers such as Plato would acknowledge female difference as a source of power and subsequently appropriate that difference and concomitant power. Also implicit in this appropriation thesis is the belief that women in fact have some mysterious creative potency that itself is a natural source of power. Robbie Kahn extends the appropriation thesis by claiming that origin myths "attack" and "dismember" the female body as they draw upon it for metaphors (1995: 4). Kahn asserts that the western tradition is self-subverting, for in "sacking birth for metaphors" this tradition acknowledges "that no descriptions of commensurate power can be derived from male experience."[6]

Although rhetorically appealing and provocative, the attempts to posit such a causal force behind Plato's patrogenesis are likely to be incomplete or reductionist. Furthermore, these causal connections are themselves related to, and often serve as the foundation for, particular political visions of feminist politics. Both O'Brien and Kahn imply that there is a deep cultural or philosophic truth about birth and reproduction that patriarchy has repressed when, in fact, there may be no such deep truth or meaning. Birth and re-production, as biological processes, have only the meaning and significance that we culturally and philosophically attach to them. To argue differently is, I believe, to commit two philosophic errors: the first is biological determinism (women give birth, therefore they have a deep, creative power that is absent in men); the second, related to the first, is cultural universalism (positing birth and reproduction as having some pan-cultural meaning when in fact we know that different cultures in different historical periods attach very different significance to these events).

The upshot of these criticisms is not that we should relegate birth to a strictly biological process, wherein it is devoid of meaning. After all, human beings are always engaged in the process of assigning meaning to the events we participate in. In this sense, human birth and reproduction have never been exclusively biological events as O'Brien has pointed out.[7] The point here is that O'Brien's appropriation thesis, as a means to explain Plato, is itself political and may lead feminist theory into an unnecessary quagmire.

As an alternative to appropriation, I suggest that it may be more productive to think of Plato's use of patrogenesis in the *Timaeus* as a theoretical fabrication. On this theory, Plato's use of birth and reproduction are entirely creative, and reflect no deep truth about the processes themselves. To be certain, he borrows the ideas of pregnancy and birth from woman. But patrogenesis reflects Plato's *wholly fabricated image of pregnancy and birth* rather than a patriarchal inversion of reality. This fabrication thesis is distinct from appropriation in a subtle but nonetheless vital way. Plato's patrogenesis is not appropriation from women precisely because appropriation requires that he acknowledge women's unique reproductive ability.[8] In the context of this dialogue at least, Plato underestimates and undervalues women's contribution. In this sense, Plato's reproductive metaphor appears to have little to do with his actual assessment of women, but rather has a lot to do with a masculine politics, even a masculine fantasy.

Exactly why Plato appeals to patrogenesis may be impossible to uncover. Plato's image of reproduction, as I have already suggested, is not the product of his own reproductive alienation. However, his masculine fantasy about reproduction may nonetheless be the result of a *perceived reproductive alienation*, which may in turn lead him to inflate and glorify the male role at the expense of the female. At the very least we can say that the images of reproduction that he does present, his characterization of reproduction as a masculine and awe-inspiring process, is his own contrivance. Plato is not robbing creative potency from woman as part of some biologically-inspired compensatory act but rather he is *fabricating the very idea of creative potency*.

Consider Plato's *Symposium*, the dialogue on Eros in which Plato puts the metaphors of pregnancy and birth to work for his epistemology. In the *Symposium*, Plato diminishes in significance women's pregnancy and birth experiences. Even in the discussion of the physical aspects of giving birth, men as well as women are depicted as pregnant and giving birth to human beings. Then, at the highest and most perfect level of Eros, *men alone* are pregnant and give birth to ideas in Beauty, the truly immortal progeny which so outshines its prototype. Plato can only simultaneously disparage all that is bodily and borrow birth for the masculine philosopher by transposing birth from the physical realm (where he thinks it is) to the metaphysical realm. In the *Symposium*, Plato demonstrates both his *abhorrence* as well as his *fantasy-like image* of what birth and pregnancy are. In one sense, nothing is more base than human reproduction. Yet, at the same time, no bodily process holds as much theoretical appeal for Plato. The image of birth that he creates is a wholly fabricated, glorified one which he manipulates with such finesse that, in the end, the material experience of birth appears as a mere imitation of the birth of metaphysical ideas in Beauty. This philosophical maneuver is not strictly an appropriation because, again, appropriation implies recognition of *what women can do*. It is this recognition that Plato does not give. Instead, he projects or transposes this image of a powerful, awe-inspiring process onto woman and simultaneously annexes it for the male for his philosophical journey of knowledge acquisition.

Returning to the *Timaeus*, we see that it too participates in a reproductive fantasy, albeit a different one from that found in the *Symposium*. The image of the power of pregnancy and birth recedes in the *Timaeus*, leaving behind only male gods, male human beings, and of course, the paternal, life-giving Forms as the originary and generative beings in the universe. Plato does equip the maternal receptacle with gestative and birthing ability, but robs these two roles of any creative or intellectual dimensions. The receptacle is not powerful but is instead passive, dimly seen, defying classification. She is mysterious and different from the paternal Forms, but not endowed with unique power comparable to the Forms.

Moreover, since women are a secondary creation, and almost incidental to reproduction in this formulation, patrogenesis makes woman irrelevant, both politically and in terms of reproduction. Like the fantasy of pregnancy and birth in the *Symposium*, this creation fantasy depicts the incredible power of life-generation, the fabricated image of creative potency. The *Timaeus* is different from the *Symposium* in that the reproductive image has lost most of its feminine dimensions, and the great creative potency stems from the male act of seed generation. Here Plato is not "sacking birth for metaphors"; rather, he taps into patrogenic embryology to depict an all-powerful process of male seed-generation. That the Greeks did not possess an advanced science of embryology in no way exculpates them for their theory of patrogenesis, as a lack of full knowledge would not necessarily lead them to conclude that women were incidental to reproduction.[9]

In the *Symposium* as in the *Timaeus*, the male role is enhanced: in the former, males are empowered with gestational and birthing ability; in the latter, the female-associated aspects of reproduction are downplayed while the act of insemination is glorified. In both cases, male creative potency is fabricated, drawing on the perceived power of the female role in reproduction and subsequently transposing it to the male. The *Timaeus* is Plato's warning to philosophic men of Athens that they should conform to a particular virtuous code that abstains from bodily desire, pleasure, and trivial emotion, regularly called "womanish." Women, for Plato, are inextricably linked to the body, unable to escape its base processes and trappings.

The *Timaeus* is also about male-empowerment through the fantasy of male creative potency. Male potency, as depicted through patrogenesis, augments Plato's project to reshape and redefine masculinity. Throughout the dialogue are references to the primacy of men in creation, to their autonomy, and to their self-sufficiency. Plato envisions men's philosophic task to be nothing short of the highest comprehension of the order and workings of the universe itself. Politically, Plato urges young men to take up the architectonic task of regenerating the *polis* in its predemocratic configuration. Such challenges require a heightened, finely tuned sort of masculinity. Only with the glorified power of self-reproduction—a power far above and beyond women's capability—will Athenian men be able to rise to the philosophic and political challenges that Plato articulates for them.

If Plato's patrogenesis and O'Brien's radical feminist version of birth and reproduction are two sides of the same coin, where does that leave us in our attempts to address the status of reproduction in western cultural discourse? On the one hand we have Plato, who fails to do justice to women's reproductive abilities but who nevertheless uses the power of reproduction as a way to speak about masculine politics. On the other hand is O'Brien, who offers us a rich and suggestive, but ultimately flawed, theory of masculine appropriation. O'Brien attempts to draw on women's experiences, but she shares with other radical feminists an uncritical celebration of female biology. She generates a new, inverted ontological argument about the sexes and reproduction: woman's role in reproduction is superior and this fact is all-important in the social relationship between men and women. O'Brien wants to suggest that women's biology has some inherent meaning—always the same, always powerful and awe-inspiring. This claim works against her other important claim that birth and reproduction are not merely physical processes but are also thinking processes. If birth and reproduction are more than base biological functions, if they are mediated by woman's consciousness, how can we argue that they have a constant, unchanging meaning? Would not the meaning of reproduction and birth vary in accordance with historical and cultural context? By arguing, as O'Brien does, that woman has an enviable, all-powerful role in reproduction, we would be committing ourselves to the view that patriarchal social relations are inevitable, that their cause lies in unchangeable facts of nature rather than in power and politics. This kind of argument is untenable and it has the effect of rendering political struggle irrelevant.

And yet, despite the problems with Plato and O'Brien and their obvious differences, there is something appealing in both of their theories. They are both drawn to the events surrounding reproduction as a source of metaphor and an object for philosophic thinking because they recognize their magnitude on the scale of human events. O'Brien compliments the ancient thinkers for their understanding of the human significance of birth—the ancients "had not 'forgotten' that beginning is birth, and that comprehension of birth process is a necessary and complex philosophical challenge" (1981: 126). In Plato and O'Brien we find an acknowledgment of the significance of birth and reproduction, even if their approaches to it are flawed.

While patrogenesis is no longer entertained as a theory of reproduction, women's experiences of birth and reproduction remain largely unarticulated even two millennia later. We need to find a way to investigate women's experiences of birth and reproduction, and to incorporate them into our cultural discourse in a way that neither lapses into a romantic, de-politicized celebration of female biology nor presupposes some deep inherent meaning that patriarchal culture has buried. If birth and reproduction do not have inherent meaning, they nevertheless have crucial significance as human events. Our cultural discourse ought to reflect rather than deny that fact.

[1]This is not to ignore the vibrant literature by women on childbirth and motherhood that does exist. But for the most part, this literature remains segregated from the larger cultural discourse of our society. Recent examples include Kline (1997) and Maushart (1999).

[2]Feminist analyses of the *Timaeus* are few in number and brief. See Tuana (1993). In a 1975 article, Geddes provides an insightful if brief analysis of

Plato's usage of patriarchal theories in embryology. Even more brief is Okin's mention of the *Timaeus*, and it too is restricted to the secondary birth of women on the earth (1979: 26).

[3]Plato, *Timaeus* in *The Collected Dialogues of Plato Including the Letters* (1961: line 42b). *Timaeus* references will hereafter be cited in the text by line number.

[4]The parallels to the Hebrew Bible are striking, as Eve, too, is a secondary creation to Adam. Eve is not a punishment but a helpmeet to Adam, and this differs from Plato's female punishment (although Eve's status as a helpmeet by no means indicates equality). However, the first story of Genesis does identify, just as the *Timaeus* does, woman as a source of shame. After the Fall, that shame comes to Eve as a punishment of pain in childbirth and subordination to Adam. In the *Timaeus*, the very existence of woman is a sign of shame, for if man had not acted intemperately, she would not have been born in the first place. One of the differences between Genesis and the *Timaeus* is that, in the former, there is a struggle over the subordination of woman—Lilith is banished to the Red Sea for her refusal to submit. In Plato's text, the inferiority of woman is presented as part of the natural ordering of the cosmos; it is not a point of struggle.

[5]Not all ancient Greeks believed that women made only a passive contribution to reproduction. However, patrogenesis was one embryological theory that achieved some currency in poetry, science, and philosophy. Notable examples include Aeschylus' *Eumenides* and Aristotle's *On the Generation of Animals*. Hippocratic writings highlighted the importance of the woman's contribution to reproduction, but they did so within a framework in which women's reproductive biology was pathologized.

[6]For further elaboration of the appropriation thesis, see duBois (1988), especially Chapter 8.

[7]Virginia Held (1993) also makes the case that to locate birth in the solely physical realm severs it from a truly human experience, and confines it to the status of animalistic processes.

[8]The critique of appropriation has its origins in David Halperin's (1990) work on the *Symposium*, in which he argues that Plato is unable to recognize the contribution of woman to reproduction. It is in response to Halperin's point that I began to conceptualize Plato's reproductive metaphor as fantasy and fabrication.

[9]As Mary Seller (1990: 224) points out, even after women's contribution was scientifically proven, there was a reluctance to abandon patrogenesis.

References

duBois, Page. *Sowing the Body: Psychoanalysis and Ancient Representations of Women*. Chicago: University of Chicago Press, 1988.

Geddes, Anne. "The Philosophic Notion of Women in Antiquity." *Antichthon: Journal of the Australian Society for Classical Studies* 9 (1975): 35-40.

Halperin, David M. "Why Is Diotima a Woman? Platonic Erós and the Figuration of Gender." *Before Sexuality: The Construction of Erotic Experience in the Ancient Greek World*. Eds. David M. Halperin, John J. Winkler, and Froma I. Zeitlin. Princeton: Princeton University Press, 1990.

Held, Virginia. *Feminist Morality: Transforming Culture, Society and Politics*. Chicago: University of Chicago Press, 1993.

Kahn, Robbie Pfeufer. *Bearing Meaning: The Language of Birth*. Urbana and Chicago: University of Illinois Press, 1995.

Kline, Christina Baker. *Child of Mine: Original Essays on Becoming a Mother*. New York: Delta, 1997.

Maushart, Susan. *The Mask of Motherhood: How Becoming a Mother Changes Everything and Why We Pretend it Doesn't*. New York: New Press, 1999.

O'Brien, Mary. *The Politics of Reproduction*. Boston: Routledge and Kegan Paul, 1981.

Okin, Susan Moller. *Women in Western Political Thought*. Princeton: Princeton University Press, 1979.

Plato. *Timaeus* in *The Collected Dialogues of Plato Including the Letters*. Eds. with Intro. and Prefatory Notes, Edith Hamilton and Huntington Cairns. New York: Pantheon Books, 1961.

Seller, Mary J. "Short Communication: Some Fallacies in Embryology Through the Ages." *The Human Embryo: Aristotle and the Arabic and European Traditions*. Ed. G.R. Dunstan. Devon: University of Exeter Press, 1990.

Tuana, Nancy. *The Less Noble Sex: Scientific, Religious, and Philosophical Conceptions of Woman's Nature*. Indianapolis: Indiana University Press, 1993.

Section III: Rethinking Feminist Politics

Rethinking Culture, Tradition, and Multiculturalism
Anti-Racism and the Politics of the Veil

Michelle Lowry

> For the colonized or "raced" subjects the notion of identity involves a loss of pre-colonial, relatively substantive forms of subjectivities through a colonizing reductionist gesture towards their historicity, multiplicity and dynamism. They become essentialized, unified or totalized as cultural entities, i.e. they undergo a reification with specifically ascribed meanings produced through the colonial negative definition of the other. (Bannerji 1995: 26)

As we enter the twenty-first century, and the population of Canada continues to become more culturally diverse, it is important that western feminists engage with cultural differences in ways that do not fall into either cultural relativist or cultural imperialist frameworks. Cultural relativism

> posits that culture is the source of [the] validity of rules and that since cultures vary, rules that are valid within one culture will not necessarily be valid in others. Thus cultural relativists elevate tolerance to a paramount value and reject the legitimacy of external critiques of culturally-based practices. (Mayer, 1994: 382)

Cultural relativism often leads to cultural essentialism, as the culture one is defending is understood as monolithic, static and ahistorical. Cultural imperialism on the other hand, occurs when "westerners" assume the superiority of "western" culture and values. Often cultural imperialists focus on the status of women in "other" societies as evidence of "western" superiority, and attempt to speak for and about those women.

I attempt to find a space in between cultural relativism and imperialism as I look at dominant understandings about Muslim women and practices of veiling in the context of Canadian multiculturalism. Muslim women are often understood by western society and western standards to be oppressed victims of their patriarchal culture and religion. This "concern" about Muslim women's oppression usually results in a "fixation on the hejab as [an] icon of the Muslim woman's identity" (Khan 1995a: 151). I believe that an anti-racist and feminist position on veiling can only be arrived at by an examination of dominant notions of culture, tradition, and community within the framework of a multicultural Canada. This process requires us to think through the ways that we understand and engage with both differences and similarities.

I am writing this paper from the location of a white, working-class, heterosexual, and able-bodied woman. Thus I take seriously Nancy Chater's concern that when white anti-racists write about issues such as veiling, they often speak or act in ways "that are based on or slide into arrogance, moralizing, self-congratulation, liberal politics, appropriation, careerism or rhetoric when conceiving of or expressing our stake in fighting racism" (1994: 100). I also take to heart Shahnaz Khan's concern that when westerners—feminist and non-feminist alike—speak about Muslim culture, they "reinforce the orientalist assumption that westerners can know the Orient better than the Orient can know itself" (1995a: 150). While it is true that in writing about racism and other cultural groups I am writing from a position of relative privilege, I do not think that these issues should only be discussed by Muslim women. The responsibility to end women's oppression is a joint responsibility, and

> to say that Third World women should take exclusive responsibility
> to analyze their situation is simply another way of marginalizing
> them. (Parashar 1993: 344)

An anti-racist feminist approach to these questions is particularly useful because anti-racism acknowledges that race, class, and gender are lived relations and not just theoretical categories (Rezai-Rashti 1994). These relations must be understood as interlocking oppressions which contribute to the invalidation of Islam in racist Canadian society and the marginalization of Muslim women in Muslim and Canadian communities (Khan 1993).[1]

Culture, Community, and Multiculturalism

When thinking about practices attributed to culture, such as veiling, it is necessary to question dominant understandings of culture and community and women's place within them. Traditionally, the dominant framework through which western scholars have understood Middle Eastern cultures is through Orientalism. Orientalism, as described by Edward Said, was the process whereby European cultures understood and imagined the Orient, and gained both strength and identity by setting themselves off against that imagined Orient (1978: 3). Orientalism homogenizes those who live in Muslim societies and those who are Muslim, de-emphasizing differences, contradictions and struggles, so that religion is seen to be the common and primary influence in people's lives (Khan 1995b). Yet, within any given culture there is struggle and difference, and this dynamism is the very thing that constitutes a culture as always changing.

Culture is not a static entity; it develops through the specific local, historical, and political realities of a society or community. Thus, it is necessary to develop an historical and political understanding of how a present culture comes to be defined and how and why certain traditions are understood as necessary for cultural expression and identity (Narayan 1998). Cultural identity does not merely reflect or represent a collection of common experiences, or a pre-ordained essence (Borsa 1990), nor do cultural traditions represent the interests of all members of a community. For example, one should look at how dominant members of society are able to discard parts of, or entire traditions and how they are able to reestablish other traditions which suit their interests. As Uma Narayan argues,

> Those with social power conveniently designate certain changes in values and practices as consonant with "cultural preservation" while designating other changes as "cultural loss" or "cultural betrayal." ...Saddling women with the primary responsibility for "cultural preservation" might remain a relative constant, even as prevailing notions of what women need to do to "preserve culture" change over time. (1998: 95)

Thus, Orientalism relies on static notions of culture, and women's place within it.

Similarly, Islamism is a system of thought that attempts to reduce the complexities and contradictions of modern society with a reductionist vision of Islam, promoting "a type of knowledge production similar to Orientalism" (Khan 1995b: 252). Within Islamic discourses, the "West" is understood as a monolithic culture, with a monolithic set of values, that must be resisted. One is left with images of a "West" that operates under one set of values, and that contains no dissent—much like Orientalist discourses about the East. These discourses set up and draw on binaries between East and West, Muslim and non-Muslim, reifying and inventing differences. And, as many feminist scholars writing about Islamism argue, in the contest over cultural meanings, identities and expression, women's bodies become understood as sites of culture and tradition—they come to represent an authentic Islamic ideal (Abu-Odeh 1992; Ayubi 1995; Khan 1995a; Peteet 1993; and Sabbah, 1984). In the Canadian context the veil can take on meanings similar to those in Islamist or Orientalist discourses, as communities try to maintain a cultural integrity via women's bodies. This also occurs when mainstream Canadian society imagines an authentic Muslim community, and an essentialized Muslim woman within that community.

As culture is a socially constructed concept embedded in relations of power, so too is the notion of community (Bannerji 1999). The ideology of multiculturalism is based on a static and ahistorical concept of ethnic culture, where a "community" is understood to be a coherent and constant entity. This community is often understood to operate under a single notion of "culture." Within this context, material issues confronting individuals in a given community are reduced to a few selected symbols of oppression such as the veil (Khan 1995b: 253). Within the framework of Canadian multiculturalism, women tend not to be viewed as individuals but as belonging to, and being part of their communities. Thus, communities are constructed in a way that downplays difference and dissent and emphasizes commonalities (Khan 1995a: 148). The category "Muslim women" appears to have a coherent and constant meaning, although women who occupy such a category may differ in sexuality, ability, age, ethnicity, race and class. Thus, their identities are understood to be primarily based on religious beliefs or affiliation.

Islamist, Orientalist, and multiculturalist discourses that understand communities as authentic or homogenous "inhibit understanding of how community alliances, and coalitions are generated and engaged in complex, contingent and contradictory relations and struggles" (Hladi 1998: 35). Such discourses posit community as homogenous, rather than as complex social groupings. Yet, communities are not free of inequitable power relations, and are a part of larger inequitable social relations within society. Thus, dominant understandings of community as homogenous are problematic and raise several important questions. Who decides what constitutes a community? On what basis do people claim membership in a community? In what ways do communities base themselves on similarities, and how do they downplay differences? Which identities are marginalized in a given community, and why?

As ethnic communities are not natural or homogenous, neither is the notion of a Canadian nation. Rather, Canada is a "construction, a set of representations, embodying certain types of political and cultural communities and their operations" (Bannerji 1997: 24). It is a country constructed on the cultural signifiers of class, gender, race, colour, language, and history. Women of colour, including Muslim women, are not part of the white dominant self definition of Canada, nor are they often understood to be Canadian. Rather, they are labeled and naturalized as visible minorities, immigrants and refugees, newcomers, illegals, aliens, foreigners, and perpetual outsiders. On top of this racialization, these women are also sexed—as women (Bannerji 1997: 25). Dominant understandings of multiculturalism as tolerance for diversity hide and/or deny the existence of racism in Canada, and elide the continuing construction of race (Srivastava 1997: 117) and the impact of gender ideologies on women of colour. Multiculturalism is vital to the process of racializing and gendering those who reside in Canada. As Himani Bannerji (1997) argues, multiculturalism racializes and centres anglo-Canadian culture as the core ethnic culture, and prides itself on tolerating other communities. If multiculturalism does manage to give "space to centre Muslim experience, it also selects those whom [constitute] its centre" (Khan 1995b: 261). And those who are centered within the Muslim community are often men. Muslim men are often seen as speaking for and about the community, while Muslim women are seen as either promoters of religious ideology or as passive recipients of that ideology (Khan 1995a).

The problems with this centering of certain individuals within a community and the static concepts that arise in the context of multiculturalism are illustrated by Goli Rezai-Rashti (1994) in her account of the experiences of minority girls in multicultural classrooms. Rezai-Rashti argues that one result of multiculturalism is a cultural relativism within the education system. For example, some parents will demand and receive special provisions for their daughters under the rubric of "culture," while requiring no special provisions for their sons. In addition, personal problems in the lives of minority female students are often uncritically chalked up to problems of sexism within their culture, rather than as symptomatic of structural racism and sexism within the educational system. Thus educators will often look to the sexist nature of a student's culture and religion and conveniently ignore the realities of sexism in Canadian society. These examples provided by Rezai-Rashti illustrate the importance of a theoretical framework which recognizes the interconnectedness of race, class, and gender in women's lives. Otherwise, one aspect of a person's life and identity, such as gender, may be prioritized or focused on, while other aspects are ignored. This is where antiracism departs from mainstream multiculturalism, as antiracism promotes egalitarianism rather than tolerance and gives more relevance to issues of class and gender. As Didi Khayatt argues, "gender as a category, when considered a basis for discrimination without accounting for class or for race, conceals distinct and intelligible levels of oppression within the category" (1994: 10). As well, Khan suggests that "practices which focus on racism without addressing sexism create a hierarchy of oppression" (1992: 53). An analysis which takes into account all aspects of a woman's identity will avoid the traps of cultural relativism and imperialism described by Rezai-Rashti, and will provide a more complex understanding of women's experiences of culture, tradition, and community.

  · Questioning and deconstructing our understandings of culture and community in the context of Canadian multiculturalism is a strategy that challenges essentialist understandings of Muslim women. If we recognize the constructed nature of Canada, the racism of official multicultural policies, and the heterogeneity of community, then women cannot be seen as belonging to a coherent category of "Muslim women"—a category seen to exist prior to entry into social relations (Narayan 1998). In other words, the category "Muslim women" should no longer have an inherent and naturalized meaning attached to it.

The ways that we understand our differences will also be challenged through this rethinking of culture and community. Narayan argues that "rather than embracing relativism, an anti-imperialist post-colonial feminist is better served by critically interrogating scripts of 'cultural difference' that set up sharp binaries between 'western' and various 'non-western' cultures" (1998: 106). We need to problematize binaries such as western/Muslim, self/other, colonizer/colonized and the essentialized differences implied in these binaries. As Susan Stanford Friedman argues, a binary opposition threatens to reproduce the "static, essentialist categories it seeks to undo" (1998: 102). As an alternative, she argues that we need to think about ways to relate across differences, and ways to theorize spaces in between difference. Otherwise, "there is the danger of affirming difference, simply as an end in itself without acknowledging how difference is formed, erased and resuscitated within and despite asymmetrical relations in power" (Grant and Sachs 1995: 99). Thus, we must restore understandings of sameness to a consideration of difference (Friedman 1998), and understand how our differences are constructed and understood from within and outside of particular locations. For Rezai-Rashti (1994), this can be accomplished by engaging in an intersubjectivity which recognizes that "our" lives are structured by similar, though not identical, economic, political, and cultural factors. Recognizing both our privilege and oppression under patriarchal, racist, class-biased, and heterosexist power relations, can lead us to a more complex understanding of our differences and similarities, and can be a basis of solidarity between women. These understandings of "similarities within our differences" (Kanpol 1995: 178) can challenge essentialist understandings of other cultures and identities, as well as our own. With these strategies in mind, I now want to turn to the politics of the veil.

Re-thinking the Veil

Dress is not a neutral action; it encodes a person's identity—their class, ethnicity, and gender (Charusheela 1996). The veil is an item of dress worn only by women, and while it is not necessarily a requirement of Islam it has become a practice associated with Muslim identity. The rhetoric of the veil can be traced to orthodox Islamic discourses which understand the female body as temptation to men and therefore hold that women should hide their bodies to ensure modesty and morality (Sabbah 1984). In doing so, a monolithic sexuality of Muslim women is constructed. The logic behind the veil assumes that women should be inconspicuous—they should hide their bodies. However, veiled women have a subjective, complicated, and shifting identity (Abu-Odeh 1992) and may wear the veil for a variety of reasons. Some women wear the hejab because they wish to neutralize their sexuality so that people will judge them by intellect rather than looks (Ahmed 1998; Haydar 1997; Manji 1995). For others, the hejab has become a visible symbol of "authenticity," and is for many a spiritual response and personal statement about identity (Khan, 1995a: 146). Others cite the veil as providing a sense of personal safety or allowing for assertiveness (Abu-Odeh 1992), while for others the donning of the veil is a symbol of anti-imperialist solidarity.

Michelle Lowry

. Whatever the reason it is important to realize that the veil as both a symbol of Muslim oppression and an icon of resistance constrains women. Thus it is necessary to resuscitate alternative experiences and meanings that the hejab holds for women and validate indigenous women's resistance to current practices (Charusheela 1996: 5). But at the same time we must not confuse anti-imperialist symbolism for anti-patriarchal struggle (Mojab 1998). We must not lose sight of the hegemonic rhetoric of the veil, nor must we ignore the racist reactions the veil elicits in Canadian society. For example, in a personal account of her experiences wearing the veil, Maysam Haydar says that people stare at her. "Their eyes get really big, occasionally their jaws will drop, and they watch my every move, trying to figure out just who I am" (1997: 44). This reaction toward a veiled woman illustrates the racism that often meets the veil, and the ways in which a veiled woman is positioned as "other."

Lama Abu-Odeh (1992) argues that the only way to point to the disempowerment of the veil is by intellectual elitism and accusations that those wearing the veil possess a false consciousness—that they do not know what is in their own interest or for their own good. Western feminists who critique practices such as the veil do not need to point to a dis/empowerment which we do not experience, or resort to accusations of false consciousness. Recognizing the racism that often accompanies veiling in a western context and recognizing the sexism rooted in the practice provides a strong feminist voice—a voice that is needed so that a "culturally sensitive approach does not remain limited to patriarchal visions of community" (Khan 1995b: 260). Western feminists should fight racism against Muslims and Muslimphobia, while being able to work with and defend Muslim women from sexism in their communities and in Canadian society as a whole. Thus I support Mojab's approach,

> which recognizes the individuality and particularity of each woman and each feminist movement, each within its specific historical context, but at the same time acknowledges that even in their uniqueness, they share common struggles against capitalist and pre-capitalist patriarchy. We can respect the voluntary choice of any woman to wear the veil, and we can oppose forcible unveiling; yet we can at the same time criticize veiling or any segregation of human beings along sex lines. (1998: 27)

As feminists learn to relate across differences, it is important that women from marginalized groups have a voice, and are heard. Borsa argues that,

> By articulating our specific experiences and representing the structural and political spaces we occupy, we offer concrete accounts of where and how we live, what is significant to our experience of cultural identity, how we have been constructed and how in turn we attempt to construct (and reconstruct) ourselves. (1990: 37)

She encourages women to voice their experiences, and perhaps more importantly calls for an understanding of how all women's experiences have been constructed in the context of unequal social relations. This understanding ensures that culture and history, and women's place in them, cannot be seen as factual, given or natural accounts, but rather as constructed. And, the myth of an "authentic" past or subject can be laid to rest. Thus, we need to "practice a critical multiculturalism that decolonizes received knowledges, histories and identities" (Mohanty 1997: xii), questioning how and why such knowledges, histories and identities are produced.

The question of the hejab is not necessarily about whether it is oppressive to women, but rather what responses does the veil elicit, and how do we understand those responses. "The contemporary controversy over the hejab needs to be viewed as an index of the social and political context in which the struggle for the hejab takes place" (Khan 1995a: 151), in the context of a racist and sexist Canadian society. Culture and traditions (such as the veil) are not inherent or natural, rather they are shaped by factors specific to a given society or "community." Thus, we must ask why certain traditions are enacted and to whose benefit and whose detriment are they enacted. Instead of focusing only on one aspect of women's identity, we must work to understand the interconnectedness of race, class, and gender in the experiences of Muslim women living in Canadian society. As Sahgal and Yuval Davis argue,

> issues of racism and sexism are intricately interwoven. However, this is no reason always to prioritize one struggle in favour of the other. The task ahead is to find ways to confront the contradictions and conflicts within minority communities as well as oppression and racism in the state and society at large. To find ways to resolve the tension between autonomy and tolerance, diversity and equality. To have the right to dissent and oppose both racism and sexism.... (1992: 25)

Michelle Lowry

I hope that the desire of feminists to work together in solidarity will be strengthened by such understandings, as will the desire to resist power, privilege, and racism within feminist movements and to resist sexism in all of its forms. Canada is an increasingly diverse nation. If feminism is to remain relevant in women's lives, feminists will need to adopt an anti-racist engagement with differences and similarities between women, and practice a politics that allows women to relate across our differences. Armed with such a framework, feminists in the twenty-first century can provide important voices in women's struggles against racism, sexism, and oppressions of all kinds.

[1]For example, a 1998 study of the representation of Islam in the Canadian media, produced by the Afghan Women's Organization, found a prevalence of Orientalist images in media coverage. Muslim women were often viewed as "other," passive, and victims, and the religion of Islam was often portrayed as violent, extreme, and radical. The author concluded that "the vilification of Muslims exceeds any other form of representation, just as the religious identity itself often supersedes any other aspects of the identity of a person who happens to be Muslim" (Jafri 1998: 18).

References

Abu-Odeh, L. "Post-colonial Feminism and the Veil: Considering the Differences." *New England Law Review* 26 (4) (Summer 1992): 1527-1537.

Ahmed, S. "American, Ambitious and Muslim." *Win Magazine* 8 (April, 1998). www.winmagazine.org/issues/issue8/win8b-htm

Ayubi, N. H. "Rethinking the Public/Private Dichotomy: Radical Islamism and Civil Society in the Middle East." *Contention* 4 (3)(Spring 1995): 79-105.

Bannerji, H. "Question of Silence: Reflections on Violence Against Women in Communities of Colour." *Scratching the Surface: Canadian Anti-Racist Feminist Thought.* Eds. E. Dua and A Robertson. Toronto: Women's Press, 1999. 261-277.

Bannerji, H. "Geography Lessons: On Being an Insider/Outsider to the Canadian Nation." *Dangerous Territories: Struggles for Difference and Equality in Education.* Eds. L. Roman and L. Eyre. New York: Routledge, 1997. 23-41.

Bannerji, H. *Thinking Through: Essays on Feminism, Marxism, and Anti-Racism.*

Toronto: Women's Press, 1995.

Borsa, J. "Towards a Politics of Location: Rethinking Marginality." *Canadian Woman Studies/les cahiers de la femme* 11 (1) Spring 1990): 36-39.

Charusheela, S. "About Dressing." *Manavi Newsletter* 8 (3) (Winter 1996): 6-8.

Chater, N. "Biting the Hand that Feeds Me: Notes on Privilege from a White Anti-Racist Feminist." *Canadian Woman Studies/les cahiers de la femme* 14 (2) (Spring 1994): 100-104.

Friedman, S.S. *Mappings: Feminism and the Cultural Geographies of Encounter*. United States: Princeton University Press, 1998.

Grant, C. A. and J. M. Sachs. "Multicultural Education and Postmodernism: Movement Toward a Dialogue." *Critical Multiculturalism: Uncommon Voices in a Common Struggle*. Eds. B. Kanpol and P. McLaren. London: Bergin and Garvey, 1995. 89-107.

Haydar, M. "Veiled?" *Hues* 2 (1) (Winter 1997): 44-45.

Hladi, J. "Power and Struggle in Educational Research: Interrogating the 'Unity' in 'Community'." *Canadian Woman Studies/les cahiers de la femme* 17 (4) (Winter 1998): 32-37.

Jafri, G. J. *The Portrayal of Muslim Women in Canadian Mainstream Media: A Community Based Analysis*. Canada: Afghan Women's Organization, 1998.

Kanpol, B. (1995). "Multiculturalism and Empathy: A Border Pedagogy of Solidarity." *Critical Multiculturalism: Uncommon Voices in a Common Struggle*. Eds. B. Kanpol and P. McLaren. London: Bergin and Garvey, 1995. 177-195.

Khan, S. "Canadian Muslim Women and Shari'a Law: A Feminist Response to Oh! Canada!" *Canadian Journal of Women and the Law* 6 (1) (1993): 52-65.

Khan, S. "The Veil as a Site of Struggle: The Hejab in Quebec." *Canadian Woman Studies/les cahiers de la femme* 15 (2, 3) (Spring/Summer, 1995a): 146-152.

Khan, S. Race, "Gender, and Orientalism: *Muta* and the Canadian Legal System." *Canadian Journal of Women and the Law* 8 (1) (1995b): 249-261.

Khayatt, D. "The Boundaries of Identity at the Intersection of Race, Class and Gender." *Canadian Woman Studies/les cahiers de la femme* 14 (2) (Spring 1994): 6-11.

Manji, I. Allah, "Lesbos and Me." *Herizons* 8 (4) (1995): 39 .

Mayer, A. M. "Universal Versus Islamic Human Rights." *Michigan Journal of*

International Law 15 (1) (1994): 308-404.

Mohanty, C. "Dangerous Territories, Territorial Power, and Education." *Dangerous Territories: Struggles for Difference and Equality in Education*. Eds. L. Roman and L. Eyre. New York: Routledge, 1997. ix-i.

Mojab, S. "'Muslim' Women and 'Western' Feminists: The Debate on Particulars and Universals." *Monthly Review* 50 (7) (December 1998): 19-30.

Narayan, U. "Essence of Culture and a Sense of History—A Feminist Critique of Cultural Essentialism." *Hypatia—A Journal of Feminist Philosophy* 13 (2) (Summer 1998): 86-106.

Parashar, A. "Essentialism or Pluralism: The Future of Legal Feminism." *Canadian Journal of Women and the Law* 6 (1) (1993): 328-345.

Peteet, J. "Authenticity and Gender: The Presentation of Culture." *Arab Women: Old Boundaries New Frontiers*. Ed. J. Tucker . Indiana: Indiana University Press, (1993). 49-61.

Rezai-Rashti, G. "The Dilemma of Working with Minority Female Students in Canadian High Schools." *Canadian Woman Studies/les cahiers de la femme* 14 (2) (Spring 1994): 76-82.

Sabbah, F. *Woman in the Muslim Unconscious*. New York: Pergamon Press, 1984.

Sahgal, Gita and Nira Yuval Davis, eds. *Refusing Holy Orders: Women and Fundamentalism in Britain*. London: Virago Press, 1992.

Said, E. *Orientalism*. New York: Vintage Books, 1979.

Srivastava, A. "Anti-Racism Inside and Outside the Classroom." *Dangerous Territories: Struggles for Difference and Equality in Education*. Eds. L. Roman and L. Eyre. New York: Routledge, 1997. 113-126.

Researching Nineteenth-Century Domestic Violence

Two Case Studies

Diane Crocker

On January 28, 1880, after a day of arguments and drinking, Catherine Sabourin attacked her husband with an axe. Several days later he died from the wounds. According to the Coroner, Octave Sabourin "came to his death under circumstances which require investigation."[1] On November 11, 1897, the *Sudbury Journal* reported that Louise Villeneuve "is one of the most melancholy mortals in the world these days. She sits by the hour with a look of most pitiable sadness in her eyes." Louise had been arrested a month earlier for the murder of her husband Felix. Their young son Aime had found his father lying in the corner of an outbuilding on their farm "covered with blood, two logs on him, and the axe sticking in his head" (*The Sudbury Journal*, October 18, 1897).

This paper recounts the nineteenth-century murder trials of Catherine Sabourin and Louise Villeneuve and explores how "not guilty" verdicts were arrived at in these two cases.[2] Both women were charged with killing their abusive husbands and their trials reveal an underlying contradiction surrounding wife assault in the nineteenth century: on the one hand, a man was allowed to violate his wife with impunity (as his property); on the other, he was expected to protect her moral superiority. This apparent contradiction is often not accounted for in our assumption that the nineteenth-century courts would not, or indeed, could not, punish wife abuse because they did not *know* that it existed.[3] They may have known that men beat their wives, but they did not *know* of *wife abuse*. Feminist legal theory has been premised on the notion that if the courts do not *know* that a problem exists, then they cannot address it and that sexist courts render sexist verdicts.

As we enter the twenty-first century, it may be time to reassess this assumption and how it has guided late twentieth-century activism. I will certainly not be arguing that the nineteenth-century courts were not sexist but the cases described in this paper illustrate that the issue is more complicated than simply a sexist court delivering sexist verdicts. The process is more complicated than we have assumed and it is affected by the contradictory discourse that existed to allow a man to violate a woman while at the same time protecting her moral superiority. In this paper, I will argue that we need to reassess some of our assumptions about how the courts operated in the past in order to find new ways to fight for suitable judicial intervention in the future.

I have used archival documents in this research as my window onto the past. Any conclusions, therefore must be tempered with concerns about how historical documents can be used to support feminist research. One problem is that documents produced by the media and the courts do not provide a full picture of women's experiences in the justice system. They were not created to serve this purpose. A second problem surrounds the preservation of historical records. It is impossible to know if the cases preserved in the archives are representative of cases tried at the time. Over the years, some files have been destroyed by accidents, others have been discarded.

Entering the twenty-first century seems like a most appropriate time to reassess the past in order to inform the future. A new wave of feminist research and theory can emerge and help direct our activist efforts in new and exciting ways. This would be useful for issues surrounding the treatment of wife abuse in the justice system but also for other issues that persist in adversely affecting women's lives. The dawn of the new century is also an appropriate time to reassess *how* we look back at the past—*how* we interpret documents produced and preserved in a different time. This paper explores these two themes, but first, it is important to describe the cases upon which this paper is based.

The Trials: *R. v. Sabourin,* 1880

In 1880 Catherine and Octave Sabourin were living in Nepean, Ontario—Octave was a heavy drinker and he was regularly abusive towards his wife and children. On January 28, 1880, Catherine Sabourin fought back at her husband one last time. In the course of a violent argument she hit him with an axe. Less than a week later, a coroner's jury passed a verdict of "wilful murder" and Catherine Sabourin was charged with killing her husband.

At the inquest, Bridget Sabourin, the eldest daughter, recounted the events leading up to her mother's fatal attack on her father. She was living with her Uncle David that winter but on January 28 she returned to her family home. Bridget described how her parents were exchanging angry words with each other as she left to pick up her younger sister at a neighbour's house. Upon returning home she found her parents and siblings in the midst of a violent brawl:

> There was only Ma and Pa and the youngest children. My to [sic] little sisters had them seperated [sic] when we came ... Lawrence [?] came with me to the door but did not go in ... Ma and Pa and the children [were] screaming ... I went into the house. Ma was in the kitchen with the wood ax. My mother told me that my father had been beating her ... he went into the kitchen and took her by the throat ... He said that there was one of them to die that night ... he had to kill her. Then he made at her and before he got to her, she gave him a blow with the ax on the back of the head.[4]

Their next eldest daughter, Julia, described her father as "very wild when drinking ... he would threaten the children as well as mother when drunk. I have known my mother to be afraid on account of the children as well as on her own account." A neighbour, Mrs. Ambrose Apps, reiterated Julia's characterization of Octave Sabourin saying that "he was a very wild man when drunk."

At the trial itself, the witnesses repeated their testimony about Octave Sabourin although Bridget changed her story about the night in question adding that her father had attacked her mother with a bottle. New witnesses at the trial included a doctor and an "expert" who described the differences between "punctured and incised wounds." According to *The Ottawa Daily Citizen* the details were "too scientific for ordinary readers" (April 24, 1880). The conclusion, however, was quite clear: Octave Sabourin died from the wounds inflicted by his wife. The point of contention was whether or not the axe was swung in self-defence or as an act of premeditated murder. The difference apparently depended upon when Catherine had fetched the axe and what her husband had been doing at the time.

The doctor who testified at the trial had come to the house to visit Octave after the fatal attack. He described another incident in which Catherine had come to see him about an injury on her lip. She told him that a colt had kicked her in the face, but upon questioning, admitted that her husband had bitten her lip during a quarrel (*The Ottawa Daily Citizen*, April 24, 1880). Catherine's lawyer emphasized this and the many other abuses and indignities that she had suffered in her marriage to Octave. In arguing for self-defence he asked the jury: "was this not sufficient to excite the passions of any human being no matter how amiable or how Christian-like a character?" (*The Ottawa Daily Citizen*, April 24, 1880).

Catherine's character was a matter of some scrutiny during the trial. Neighbours described her as a good, honest, and peaceful woman. The newspaper portrayals suggested that she was either mentally unstable or simply incapable of understanding what was going on. Her daughters were similarly portrayed:

> Mrs. Sabourin did not fully realize the gravity of her situation. She was quite calm and took but little interest in the evidence. The two elder daughters appear as though nothing out of the ordinary had occurred and in describing the details of the terrible butchery did not evince the slightest emotion. (*The Ottawa Daily Citizen*, February 3, 1880)

The newspaper also reported that Catherine was victimized both by her husband's brutality and by his influence. Over the course of their life together Catherine had apparently taken to drinking heavily. The newspaper reported her lawyer's description of how Octave had led Catherine down a path of depravity:

> when the prisoner married [the] deceased she was a sober woman, but through his influence and at times brutal conduct, was forced to drink what was at first an abhorrence to her, but afterwards became a strong appetite, which she could not resist.[5]

Catherine's inability to resist temptation reinforced a notion that she was helpless. As the trial proceeded this was reflected in the newspaper descriptions and they changed their tone: "She was dressed in black, and during most of the time her face was veiled ... [she] appeared to watch the case very closely" (*The Ottawa Daily Citizen*, April 25, 1880).

In the Judge's charge to the jury, he acknowledged "domestic infelicity" but most of his comments focussed on the fact that Octave did die from wounds inflicted by his wife. Apparently unimpressed by any notion of "self-defence," he advised the jury to consider the differences between "murder, manslaughter and mere circumstance." In the end, the jury returned a verdict of "not guilty" and Catherine Sabourin was set free.

R. v. *Villeneuve*, 1897

A headline on October 21, 1897 in *The Sudbury Journal* read: "BRUTAL MURDER! In the Township of Rayside." Felix Villeneuve had been found dead in an outbuilding on his farm. The jury at the inquest into his death stated:

> that we find that [the] deceased came to his death as a result of wound inflicted on the head with an axe which we believe was in the hands of deceased's wife when the wounds were inflicted. We further are of opinion that the immoral life of Arthur Chartrand and Mrs. Villeneuve was the cause of the murder. (*The Sudbury Journal*, October 28, 1897)

At the inquest, most of the evidence was provided by the Villeneuve's young son, Aime. At around noon, on the day of his father's death, Aime set out to plough the fields. He stated that "Father and mother were talking when I went away. When going to the field I looked back and saw mother going to the house" (*The Sudbury Journal*, October 28, 1897). Aime said that about half an hour later he wandered into the outbuilding where his father was working and found him, lying dead. He said that he fetched his mother and:

> She went with me to the building. She told me to get some water but I was afraid to go alone, and we both went and got some water from the house. Mother wiped father's face ... she then said we would go get some help from the neighbours ... I then went to Delphise [?] Chartrand's where Arthur and Phillias were at work and they went back, Arthur running very fast.... (*The Sudbury Journal*, October 28, 1897)

During the trial the media questioned Aime's testimony. He claimed that he would have seen his mother had she left the house but a newspaper report called this testimony "absurd" because of the layout of the land and the buildings. This point was hotly debated during the trial and there are several maps included in the case file that were presumably used as evidence. In terms of a motive for the murder, newspaper reports focussed their attention on

Arthur Chartrand, "a somewhat noted character . . who is generally believed to have been on too intimate terms with the wife of the deceased" (*The Sudbury Journal*, October 21, 1897). Arthur was further incriminated by John Hammel who claimed to have heard Arthur threaten to kill Felix Villeneuve. The witness did not, however, admit to knowing about any kind of relationship between Arthur and Louise.

The newspaper reports neglected to address the fact that Louise had charged her husband with assault several months prior to his death. The case file includes a copy of the statement that Louise had provided to police at that time. In her statement she alluded to some kind of debt that Felix owed Chartrand:

> My husband was drunk and began to play with me. He asked me if I ever slept with Chartrand? I said no. My husband then pushed me along to the bed and told me he had made a good bargain with Chartrand about the notes. He would make him earn the note. I told him I would not allow him to make any bargain.... My husband began to play with me and raised my dress up. He also called Chartrand into the room. I called on Chartrand to take my husband away. Chartrand took him away from me.[6]

The newspaper reports also focussed on Aime's testimony that his mother and father had not fought much since she had had him arrested (*The Sudbury Journal*, October 28, 1897) and on the supposed infidelity as the source of their conflicts:

> It is known that deceased and his wife have had a good deal of trouble among themselves for some time past, one cause of which is said to have been the frequent visits of Chartrand to the home of the murdered man. (*The Sudbury Journal*, October 21, 1897)

Apparently, however, the judge accepted Aime's depiction of the events on the day of his father's death. He charged the jury in favour of a "not guilty" verdict. On December 3, after two hours of deliberation, the jury decided that Louise had not murdered her husband but the editors of *The Sudbury Journal* did not agree. One newspaper article suggested that no effort had really been made to convict the prisoner and hastened to add that two members of the jury had held out for a conviction.

Discussion

One question raised by these two cases is: How did the verdicts come about? The verdicts are unexpected because we assume that the nineteenth-century courts would not have allowed female defendants any benefit of the doubt. We also assume that because the courts did not *know* that *wife abuse* existed, they would not have been able to account for it in their verdicts. These cases call these assumptions into question and the outcomes of the Sabourin and Villeneuve trials seem remarkably progressive. It is remarkable to think that the courts recognized that these women were abused by the men that they purportedly killed and that this was somehow considered by the court and the jury as a relevant information. The question is, if they did not *know* that *wife abuse* existed, then how could they make allowances for it?

The "not guilty" verdict in Catherine Sabourin's case is interesting because it is quite clear that her husband died from the wounds that she inflicted. Given the misogynist nineteenth-century judiciary, we would have expected her to have been found guilty regardless of any mitigating circumstances or self defence arguments. Self defence arguments, in cases of women who kill abusive spouses, have only recently come to be officially accepted by the courts. It may be pushing the interpretive limits to suggest that the jury thought about the incident as involving self defence but they obviously accepted that it was "mere circumstance" (as the judge suggested) and in their verdict they somehow accounted for the insufferable conditions endured by Catherine Sabourin. In the case of Louise Villeneuve, it is difficult to understand how the case got to trial in the first place considering Aime's testimony. There is nothing that indicates on what grounds the coroner's inquest implicated Louise. Her purported affair is the only motive provided and that points towards Chartrand as the murderer, not Louise. The verdict is unexpected because she was implicated in the first place so there is no reason to think that she would not have been found guilty. Did the jury feel sympathetic towards her, despite the supposed affair, given the abusive nature of her husband?

The feminist literature on the judicial system argues that wife abuse is not taken seriously by the courts and that female defendants are punished for their transgression of gender expectations rather than for the crime they may have committed. Feminist criminologists have studied female offenders and how they are treated in the court system (e.g., Adelberg and Currie 1987; Bickle 1991; Chesney-Lind 1986; Daly 1994; Wight and Meyers 1996). A lot of this work is aimed at counteracting the misogynist assumptions of earlier research (Smart 1979). One early criminology text, for example, described female offenders as having a "masculine streak" (von Hentig qtd. in Potter 1995). This demonstrates the prevailing attitude that it is not conceivable for a "normal" woman to commit a crime. According to Ballinger (1996) female offenders are deemed to be either "mad" or "bad." "Bad" women are apparently treated harshly because, not only did they commit a crime, they also contravened gender role expectations. Ballinger (1996) argues that they are punished for both transgressions. "Mad" women, on the other hand, have fallen victim to their weak feminine constitution. Ballinger (1996) suggests that the courts pity their plight as women and deliver light sentences based on the shortcomings of their gender rather than the severity of their crime. Ballinger (1996) suggests that a third label, "victim," has been the only alternative to the mad/bad dichotomy. The female "victim" who is charged has not contravened her gender role expectations so the label of victim is a way to show that she, like other women, is unable to protect herself. All of these labels perpetuate inappropriate stereotypes about women and they sanction misogynist judicial decision making.

Along these same lines, Constance Backhouse (1991a) has described the situation for women in the nineteenth century who were charged with infanticide. Her research suggests that the courts were lenient and acquitted many young and unmarried women who had been charged with killing a newborn child. Backhouse (1991a) notes that the male judiciary saw these actions as rational and even honourable under the circumstances: "up to two thirds of the courts were issuing outright acquittals of women who were charged with murder or manslaughter" (Backhouse 1991b: 20-1). In a sense, these young women, and their "mad" sisters, were viewed in a similar light. Both were maintaining the gender status quo.

Ballinger's (1996) typology for female offenders applies to the depictions the two women described in this paper. Catherine Sabourin was portrayed as both a victim and as somewhat "mad." Her husband had badly abused her and also led her down the road of alcoholism. Since this contravened her "Christian-like" character, she was clearly not mentally fit or able to preserve her own identity. These factors may have induced the verdict of "not guilty." Catherine Sabourin caused the death of her husband but she had not contravened gender role expectations. While this may have worked in her favour, it is still a form of judicial misogyny and it reinforces negative female stereotypes.

Judicial bias is probably what brought the case against Louise Villeneuve to trial despite the lack of evidence. She was considered "bad" from the outset—as indicated by her supposed extra-marital affair. According to this we would have expected her to have been found guilty. As a "bad" woman, she was guilty of an offence regardless of whether or not she killed her husband. However, it seems that this discourse did not prevail because there was simply no evidence to prove that she had swung the axe. Either that or perhaps the jury felt sympathetic to her plight and the fact that she had endured an abusive husband. Her affair may have motivated the prosecution but it may have been her husband's bad behaviour that swung the pendulum towards a not guilty verdict. Louise may or may not have killed her husband and she may or may not have been having an affair with Chartrand. These "facts" are less important than her depiction in the newspaper as an adulteress. For all intents and purposes she is what she was depicted as being. This is a "fact" of all historical representations. She went to trial depicted as a adulteress but perhaps she was acquitted as a battered woman.

This interpretation of the Sabourin and Villeneuve trials may be going too far. The point is that these cases contravene our assumptions in interesting ways. If Catherine Sabourin was considered "mad" then this may explain her acquittal. The self defence argument presented by her lawyer is, however, completely unexpected and cannot be accounted for in our assumptions about the nineteenth-century judicial system. Louise Villeneuve could have been found guilty because of the biases established against her and her supposed affair. In both of these cases, a sexist judiciary somehow overcame the biases that feminists have noted. This does not mean that the rationales for the two acquittals was not sexist or paternalistic, simply that this is a complex process informed by apparently contradictory discourses on marriage, family, and femininity. On the one hand, women were viewed as mindless pieces of property, incapable of achieving high intellectual standards or being involved in the public sphere. On the other hand, women were viewed as morally superior to men, better at educating children and raising them to be upstanding citizens, and even important educators of men. A nineteenth-century manual for young married women depicts men as brutes that women must guide into a more civilized life (Alcott 1873). These contradictory discourses appear to have affected judicial decision making in unexpected ways, producing what amount to desirable outcomes for the women charged with murdering their husbands. We have generally not accounted for these types of contradictions in our analyses of the nineteenth-century courts.

Diane Crocker

This leads to questions about the use of such historical documents as a means of interpreting the past and using its lessons to address issues in the present. The documents used in this research are "official" in the sense that they were compiled by court officials or written in newspapers. The main source of information on these cases came from Criminal Indictment Files that were compiled by the Crown Attorney. The Files contain documents such as police reports, inquiry verdicts, and arrest warrants but they are quite discrepant. The Sabourin and Villeneuve files contained a variety of information including witness statements. The media reports consisted of a day-by-day account of the events in court but they also included commentaries on the outcomes. Both of these cases attracted a lot of media attention.

When looking at official documents, Natalie Davis (1987: viii) suggests that we must "understand the rules for their creation." Court records were created to maintain a record of testimony and evidence, not to shed light on the lives of the people involved. The media reports tended either to simply provide an unedited narrative describing the sequence of events in court, or to provide a forum for the newspaper editors opinions on the matter. In either case, these documents were not created in order to allow us a window on the lived experiences and realties for those involved. As Constance Backhouse suggests, "studying the legal records of a white supremacist, patriarchal regime is not well calculated to unearthing much of relevance about the lives of women" (1991a: 6). This is particularly true for the types of documents used in this research. They provide almost no insight into how Catherine Sabourin and Louise Villeneuve interpreted the events or the outcomes.

A second issue relating to the use of archival documents for feminist research lies in the rationale behind their preservation —which records were kept and why? Keith Jenkins (1995) refers to this as the "historicised nature of the records." The historicised nature of the documents used in this research involves a process of preservation and collection that is probably more related to bureaucratic or accidental, rather than patriarchal, processes. That is, there was probably no systematic attempt to preserve records by any sexist-based selection process. Having said that, it is possible that the Villeneuve and Sabourin cases were preserved because of the unusual nature of the charge. Perhaps one of the Court clerks thought that the file was worth saving, perhaps the file happened to be in a box that was not destroyed by fires or otherwise lost. Whatever the case, it is impossible to determine how representative these, or any other extant cases, really are.

Conclusion

The problems associated with archival research leave us looking back at the past into a distorted mirror. It is therefore difficult to interpret and even more difficult to pick out the subtleties of various situations under investigation. We have always assumed that the mirror is distorted in ways that obscures women's lives but as I have shown in this paper, the distortion may take a slightly different form than we expect. There are several ways to interpret the cases described in this paper, but there is one thing for certain—the cases reveal a more complicated picture than we have previously assumed.

The question is, if, in the nineteenth century, they did not *know* that *wife abuse* existed, then how could they make allowances for it in judicial decisions? The answer to this question lies in understanding that the intersection of discourses can have unanticipated outcomes and that our view on the past must account for this. To answer that question goes beyond the scope of the small research project described in this paper, however, it points to issues that we should consider as we push feminist research, theory, and activism into the twenty-first century.

This leads to another interesting question about the twentieth century: since we knew that wife abuse is a crime, did the practice of punishment actually reflect a discourse of liberation for women or a lagging paternalism from the nineteenth century? In other words, could we have been getting better outcomes for the wrong reasons? This is an important question because the answer could change the way in which we push for judicial reform. Feminist research and activism have revolved around the assumption that a sexist judiciary will inevitably and invariably produce sexist outcomes. This paper calls this assumption into question and suggests that the process is not this straightforward. It is therefore possible that the criminal justice reforms advocated by feminists *could*, at worst, reinforce, at best leave intact, sexist and paternalistic decision making.

Wife abuse had no name in the nineteenth century. The twentieth century witnessed its naming as a serious social problem. Feminist researchers and activists have been very successful in their fight to put the problem on the public agenda. There have been gains in the judicial system but it seems that things have come to a bit of a standstill. Despite the education of judges and lawyers, and the creation of specific policies on wife abuse, the judicial system has not had the effect that many feminists hoped it would. For this reason, it seems like an appropriate time to assess our assumptions and develop a revised agenda in our fight against wife abuse in the twenty-first century. We should aim, in this new century, to have judicial outcomes that work for women and that were supported by discourses of liberation.

[1]Criminal Indictment Files, Ontario Provincial Archives, RG-22-393 box 16.
[2]A more detailed account of the legal cases described in this paper appears in another paper entitled "Of Trials, Tribulations and Truths: Researching Nineteenth Century Spousal Homicide" in *Policing the New Millennium: Critical Essays on Social Control* York University Critical Criminology Association (eds.) Toronto: Centre for Police and Security Studies, Atkinson College, York University (1997).
[3]This assumption is apparent in writing emerging from the "discovery" of wife abuse in the 1970s. See for example Dobash and Dobash (1979).
[4]Criminal Indictment Files, Ontario Provincial Archives, RG-22-393 box 16. Unless otherwise indicated, all the information on the Sabourin case comes from this source.
[5]This is based on testimony provided by two neighbours at the trial as reported in *The Ottawa Daily Citizen*, April 24, 1880.
[6]Criminal Indictment Files, Ontario Provincial Archives, RG-22-393 box 1.

References

Adelberg, Ellen and Claudia Currie, eds. *Too Few to Count: Canadian Women in Conflict with the Law* Vancouver: Press Gang Publishers, 1987.

Alcott, William A. *The Young Wife or Duties of Woman in the Marriage Relation* New York: Arno Press, 1972 (1873).

Backhouse, Constance. *Petticoats and Prejudice: Women and the Law in Nineteenth Century Canada* Toronto: Women's Press, 1991a.

Backhouse, Constance. *Women and the Law in Nineteenth Century Canada* Winnipeg: Canadian Legal History Project, 1991b.

Ballinger, Anette. "The Guilt of the Innocent and the Innocence of the Guilt: The Cases of Marie Fahmy and Ruth Ellis." *No Angels: Women who Commit Violence.* Eds. Alice Meyers and Sarah Wight . San Francisco: Pandora Books, 1996. 1-28.

Bickle, Gayle S. and Ruth Peterson. "The Impact of Gender-Based Family Roles on Criminal Sentencing" *Social Problems* 38(3) (1991): 372-394.

Chesney-Lind, Meda. "Women and Crime: The Female Offender." *Signs*

12(1) (1986): 78-96.

Daly, Kathleen. *Gender, Crime and Punishment* New Haven: Yale University Press, 1994.

Davis, Natalie. *Fiction in the Archives: Pardon Tales and Their Tellers in Sixteenth Century France* Stanford, CA: Stanford University Press, 1987.

Dobash, R. Emerson and Russell P. Dobash. *Violence Against Wives: The Case Against the Patriarchy* New York: Routledge, 1979.

Jenkins, Keith. *On What is History? From Carr and Elton to Rorty and White* London: Routledge Press, 1995.

The Ottawa Daily Citizen, April 25, 1880.

The Ottawa Daily Citizen, April 24, 1880.

The Ottawa Daily Citizen, February 3, 1880.

Smart, Carol. "The New Female Criminal: Reality or Myth?" *British Journal of Criminology* 19 (1) (1979): 50-59.

The Sudbury Journal, October 28, 1897.

The Sudbury Journal, October 21, 1897.

The Sudbury Journal, October 18, 1897.

Potter , C. B. "I'll Go to the Limit and Then Some: Gun Moles, Desires and Danger in the 1930s." *Feminist Studies* 21(1) (1995): 41-66.

Wight, Sarah and Alice Myers, eds. *No Angels: Women Who Commit Violence* San Francisco: Pandora Books, 1996.

On the Edge of Connection

Global Feminism and the Politics of the Internet

Krista Hunt

On the edge of the millennium, feminists are paying close attention to the Internet—as a powerful cultural space and an important political tool. When surfing through academic, activist, hard copy, and home-page information sources, questions arise about what place the Internet has for feminism, and vice versa. More specifically, what role will the Internet play in the "global women's movement" and how are feminists on-line shaping and re-shaping what the "global women's movement" is (imagined to be)? In this article, I examine various ways women's groups are using the Internet to organize globally, how these groups locate themselves vis à vis feminism, and how postmodern conceptions of global feminism may provide a basis to re-think identity politics and, importantly, political practice. These questions stem from larger debates with which feminists on the edge of the millennium must grapple. Is a global women's movement possible in light of debates over essentialism, solidarity, difference, etc? And can the Internet be a tool in a global women's movement when most women are not connected? These are the questions that frame this paper.

Feminist Thought on the Edge

Located on the edge of the millennium, feminists are able to simultaneously look back on the history of feminist thought and look forward to future feminisms. Feminist theory has evolved from liberal feminist[1] preoccupations with proving that women and men are equal, and radical feminist[2] contentions that women are essentially different than men. While these theories make uncontested contributions to the development of feminist thought, and are still widely used theoretical models, both perspectives have ignored the differences between women in their respective focus on equality with men or difference from men. Critiques from women whose voices and experiences are marginalized—women from the third world, poor women, women of colour, lesbians—have forced feminists to assess "who *we* are" and "what *we* are fighting for". These tensions have caused some women to question whether they are feminists when their lives and experiences are invisible(see Calhoun 1997; hooks 1981), as well as raising questions about whether we are "women" at all (Riley 1988).

These tensions within identity politics between the primacy of gender identity and the recognition of difference frame conceptions of feminist organizing. Questions about "how feminists can organize" in light of the vast differences between them have, on the one hand, sparked calls to focus on the similarities in the name of solidarity, and on the other, to form coalitions through these differences. Since these theoretical questions affect the form of political practice, addressing them is essential for projects concerned with feminist organizing on a global scale. As such, this exploration into the place of the Internet for global feminist organizing is located within these larger debates.

Global Feminisms

In order to contextualize these articulations of "global feminism" on-line, it is important to revisit different conceptions of global feminism—specifically, the basis for unity/coalition building. Chilla Bulbeck lists three common articulations of foundations upon which to build coalitions: (1) unity based on our identity as women and the fight against patriarchal oppression; (2) the recognition of differences between women within a movement based on the belief that the oppression of women is the major struggle; (3) movements that are based around multiple struggles including women's issues (Bulbeck 1988). While these visions can be characterized as an historical progression within feminism, it is important to note that all of these visions continue to be articulated, critiqued and debated in theory and practice.

The first vision of global feminism, which I will refer to as the "universal sisterhood" model, has as its basic assumption that women around the world are sisters in a common struggle. This has been critiqued for its essentialism, its ignorance of the differences between women including issues of race, class, sexuality, nationality, age, occupation, and ability, and its dualistic thinking about oppressors and oppressed (men vs. women). Since the differences between women are unacknowledged, the privilege and power that some women enjoy at the expense of others (class or race privilege are good examples) lead to an uneasy alliance. Issues including the marginalization of certain groups of women within feminism, the silencing of their voices, the colonization of other women's experience, and the objectification of "third world women" have been raised. These issues require continued articulation in order to clarify the contradictions within feminism.[3] This type of feminism has also been criticized for putting women in the position of having to make the choice to align themselves with women at the expense of their solidarity with men in other political struggles (Bulbeck 1988: 147). Jacqui Alexander and Chandra Talpade Mohanty argue that conceptions of transnational feminism most often originate in the West and are based on "a notion of universal patriarchy operating in a transhistorical way to subordinate all women" (1997: xix). As such, because of this vision, many women have expressed alienation from western feminism of this sort and resist using the feminist label.

The second vision, which is most accurately described as the "add difference and stir" model, recognizes (through these critiques by other women) that there are differences between women around the world, but still contends that for all women, gender oppression is the most important struggle. This perspective makes two problematic assumptions: it creates a hierarchy of oppression and analytically separates the workings of sexism from those of racism, heterosexism, or capitalism. In so doing, one's multiple identities are assumed to be experienced to varying degrees and in distinguishable ways depending on a particular situation, instead of as a complex web of identities that may be both privileging and oppressive simultaneously.

The third category, which is most promising for coalition building among many social movements, is properly termed the "social movement coalition" model. It addresses multiple identities and issues that women struggle with: issues that are similar for women around the world (e.g. violence against women); particular issues that women share with members of their local communities—including men (e.g. land claims); and issues that position different groups of women in opposition to one another (e.g. colonialism). For Bulbeck, "[c]oalition work certainly does not advocate incorporation of the other. It means walking the tightrope of connection, distance and power" (1988: 221). However, the fear for some feminists is that the issues specific to women will be subsumed under the banner of issues like nationalism or socialism, and ultimately, women's issues will (once again) be marginalized.

Of course, these are only a sample of various models of feminist theory/ practice. Alternative conceptions of the basis for coalitions have also been imagined which question fundamental tenets of feminism. For instance, Donna Haraway is concerned about feminist identity politics and the problems associated with universal, totalizing theories. She argues that feminists must embrace the ambiguities and contradictions of partiality and indeterminancy. Her model for this is that of the cyborg—a "myth about transgressed boundaries, potent fusions, and dangerous possibilities which progressive people might explore as one part of needed political work" (1991: 154). Cyborg feminists resist previous models of unity and sisterhood and do not attempt to create grand narratives since "single vision produces worse illusions than double vision or many-headed monsters" (1991: 154). Haraway's "is a dream not of a common language, but a powerful infidel heteroglossia. It is an imagination of a feminist speaking in tongues to strike fear into the circuits of the super-savers of the new right. It means both building and destroying machines, identities, categories, relationships, space stories" (1991: 181).

Similarly, Judith Butler raises questions about grand narratives. She asks, "[d]o the exclusionary practices that ground feminist theory in a notion of "women" as subject paradoxically undercut feminist goals to extend its claims to "representation?" (1990: 5). Butler argues that the unity of gender is an effect of power which not only "presumes, fixes and constrains the very 'subjects' that it hopes to represent and liberate," (1990: 148) but also reinforces compulsory heterosexuality which depends on fixed oppositional sex/gender identities. Paradoxically, through the reification of identity, feminism becomes a regulatory practice under the guise of liberation. Since the prerequisite of unity for politics comes at a price (exclusion and regulation), the question is about whether unity is, in fact, necessary in order to act (1990: 14-15).

For Butler, "there need not be a 'doer behind the deed,' but that the 'doer' is variably constructed in and through the deed" (1990: 142). In other words, coalition building need not search for a unifying identity, but can act within existing contradictions. Thus, an "antifoundationalist approach to coalition politics assumes neither that 'identity' is a premise nor that the shape or meaning of a coalitional assemblage can be known prior to its achievement"

(1990: 15). What becomes politicized is the process of signification. Since identities become intelligible through a process of repetition—we are not women, but always in the process of becoming women— agency lies with the possibility of doing things differently. As such, "[t]he task is not whether to repeat, but how to repeat or, indeed, to repeat and, through a radical proliferation of gender, to displace the very gender norms that enable the repetition itself" (1990: 148).

What is interesting about Haraway's (1991) and Butler's (1990) visions is that they not only respond to the problems of unity and difference, but also question feminisms that create grand narratives about patriarchy, "women," and oppression. They argue that feminists must embrace and act within the differences and contradictions. Included in this argument is the necessity to act collectively while resisting the reification of identity, and to embrace the possibilities that can result from indeterminancy, contradiction, and transgressed boundaries. According to Haraway, "[c]yborg writing is about the power to survive, not on the basis of original innocence, but on the basis of seizing the tools to mark the world that marked them as other" (1991: 1975). The debate is no longer about whether or not to use the Master's tools, because we cannot step outside of mechanisms of power. Therefore, if tools like the Internet can be subverted for the purposes of feminism, the question becomes, how will feminists use this tool to imagine and create alternative futures?

Butler's gender fables(1990: xi) and Haraway's science fiction (1991: 149) illustrate how feminists have created fictions which masquerade as fact. While debates continue and new coalitions are imagined and built, it is clear that concepts such as "women," "feminism," or "unity"—which serve as the foundation for many conceptions of global feminism—are "in trouble." However, perhaps this trouble is important and productive. In theory and practice, on-line and off-line, visions of global feminism are being articulated which are inevitably partial, and thus reflect the insufficiency of singular issues, singular identities, and singular visions. Can these examples of multiplicity and indeterminancy be the beginning of new images of global feminism on and off-line? Specifically, are there examples of Butler's antifoundational approach, or Haraway's powerful infidel heteroglossia being imagined?

Feminism and the Internet

Reports about the dangers of the Internet abound—from sexual predators stalking innocent children in chat rooms to anti-abortion extremists creating hit-lists of abortion doctors. In the same breath, we hear analyses from the optimists: like Nicholas Negroponte's (1996) technotopic fable about the totalizing power of technology and the possibilities that await users/consumers, or Sadie Plant's tale (1997) of "genderquakes" and the cultural shifts taking place through new technologies which will ultimately transfer power from men to women. When taken together, interesting contradictions, holes and inconsistencies arise; dangers and possibilities are simultaneously expressed. It is here, within the tensions that foreclose singular conclusions about the effects and possibilities of the Internet, that we must think and act.

One of the most promising aspects of the Internet is the potential for social movements to harness this technology for social action and justice both online and (more importantly) off-line. We have witnessed the political power of the Internet for the Zapatistas[4] and more recently as an organizational tool for anti-globalization protests in Seattle and Washington.[5] For women's groups, the Internet was an important tool for communication during the Fourth World Conference on Women and the NGO Forum on Women 1995 in Beijing, China.[6] It has continued to develop as a tool for feminist communication, publication, networking, education, action, and research. The Internet is also undoubtedly a developing cultural space that feminists can contribute to building. Some feminist groups, like Virtual Sisterhood,[7] are working to achieve on-line goals such as full access and technical training for women. Others are interested in using the Internet as a tool for urgent campaigns "off-line," like RAWA's website[8] that publicizes the situation of women in Afghanistan. In important ways, feminists are linking virtual realities and real lives, but issues of access are of primary concern.[9]

The promise of the Internet is hampered because of the reality that the majority of people, let alone a majority of women, do not have access to this technology. Access to Internet technology not only requires money to buy hardware and software, but also access to a telephone,[10] a reliable telecommunications infrastructure, affordable connection fees, proficiency in English and tech-language, the desire to "get connected," technical support, the ability and desire to express oneself through text. Even if these things exists, many women still require "a room of one's own" and the time to invest. As well, even with access to this technology, energy has to be channeled into making information accessible. This includes the translation of information into other languages and the organization of information in order to reduce the amount of time (and money) spent searching for information on-line.[11] Even those who could have Internet access often choose not to pursue it, do not understand or value it, or feel too alienated to use it. In many ways, the Internet can pose serious challenges in terms of skill sets and ways of communicating/knowing. For many, the Internet remains generationally, linguistically, culturally, and class specific.

An examination of the Global List of Women's Organizations highlights the significance of the issue of access for feminist organizing on-line.[12] This analysis was conducted in order to get some sense of which countries had women's organizations with websites. Since the Global List is one of the most comprehensive sites dedicated to maintaining a list of women's organizations world-wide, as well as organizations that have women's programs, it serves as a representative sample. The organizations listed include universities, libraries, bookstores, governmental organizations, NGOs, religious groups, health services, advocacy groups, fundraising groups, and crisis centres. They range from a local/regional to a national and global focus. Denise Osted, the women responsible for creating and maintaining this list, explicitly states that the list is meant to be representative of groups from around the world, not just Europe and North America.

Most of the organizations listed do not have websites. In terms of organizations with homepages, American groups have more websites than those located in all other countries combined (see appendix A). It is not surprising that virtually all nations with more than a handful of connected organizations are from the North. The Global List illustrates the vast differences in Internet use between countries around the world. Clearly, when conceptualizing the role of the Internet for global feminist organizing, we must keep in mind issues of access and how to bridge existing gaps. Issues of access affect not only who can get connected, but also what issues, visions, and voices are visible, and the sorts of coalitions that can be forged beyond the Internet.

Feminism(s) On-line

With issues of access in mind, it is important to examine how women's groups are using the Internet to organize globally, and specifically to analyze how these groups define themselves and their political objectives. To do so, I conducted an analysis[13] of Internet sites identified as being concerned with global feminist issues.[14] I discovered these sites through search engines, feminist on-line databases, hard copy publications on feminism and the Internet, feminist list-serves, and often by accident. By virtue of the (dis)organization of the Internet, it is safe to assume that there are numerous sites that I have not encountered, and because of space restrictions, many more that I have not included. What *Women for Women*, the *Sisterhood is Global Institute*, and the *Coalition for Global Solidarity and Social Development* represent are examples of the various ways feminists are addressing international or global issues, how the Internet is an important tool for these projects, and how feminists on-line imagine and contribute to multiple articulations of a "global feminist" movement.

Women for Women,[15] an "international," humanitarian, non-profit organization, is dedicated to creating awareness about the situation of women in Bosnia Herzegovina, Croatia, Rwanda, and Kosovo, and to providing personal, economic, and educational support to survivors of the wars. The *Sisterhood is Global Institute*[16] (SIGI) is a global organization dedicated to educating women about their human rights and uses the Internet to reach women around the world and distribute action alerts in "real time." The *Coalition for Global Solidarity and Social Development*[17] has been organized around the World Summit for Social Development+5 in order to foster grassroots participation in the Summit, to provide a network for groups involved in global issues including social, political and economic development and human security at the beginning of the twenty-first century. This coalition is concerned with the simultaneous processes of increasing quality of life for many and the growing inequality between rich and poor. Specifically, it is interested in how globalization and new technologies are contributing to these processes. Included in the goals of the coalition is the consideration of gender issues.

What these groups illustrate is the diversity of organizations using the Internet to facilitate work on feminist issues and objectives. An important distinction between these three groups is the basis for solidarity/unity. Both *Women for Women* and the *Sisterhood is Global Institute* organize around women's oppression and recognize (either implicitly or explicitly) that women around the world do not experience this in the same way. However, while they can both be characterized as recognizing the differences between women around the world, they consider the oppression of women to be primary. Thus, *Women for Women* and the *Sisterhood is Global Institute* fit well within the "add difference and stir" model of global feminism in terms of their focus on women while recognizing diversity.

The *Coalition for Global Solidarity and Social Development* differs from these two groups because it organizes around global problems—like poverty and violence—which affect many people around the world. This organization is based on multiple struggles, of which women's issues are a part. It is implicit that these activists coalesce around their commitment to these issues, rather than on unity through common identity. Therefore, the *Coalition for Global Solidarity and Social Development* can be characterized as an articulation of the "social movement coalition" model and contributes to a focus on issues above and beyond the nation-state, including women's issues.

Another difference between these groups is the language used to identify each organization, particularly in relation to the issues they deem most relevant. Implicit in the use of language is the politics of using different labels. *Women for Women* identifies itself as "an international humanitarian organization" run by women for women. *Women for Women* does not adopt the term feminist or feminism, which may stem from issues of alienation discussed earlier. In contrast, SIGI uses women and feminist/ism somewhat interchangeably. *Global Solidarity* also uses the discourse of women and gender without clear differentiation. In thinking about how feminism is conceptualized online, it is important to remember the debates over the use of "gender" versus "women." [18] We must also be mindful of the reasons certain organizations working for women do not adopt a feminist label[19] and how these issues point to the problems associated with creating grand (or, in some cases, "global") narratives about women, or feminism.

The use of "global" versus "international" is another notable distinction. "International" usually refers to the actions of and between states, whereas a focus on global relations also includes the role of NGOs, social movements and transnational corporations.[20] *Women for Women* is an "international" organization. This relates to its focus on the condition of women within particular nation-states around the world. SIGI uses both international and global, possibly because of its focus on Human Rights and the tension between global conceptions of human rights and the realization of those universal rights within particular nation-states. *Global Solidarity* uses the term "global" for many reasons. In response to the "lack of any significant attempt or openness to encourage NGO participation in Geneva,"[21] global is used instead of international to stress the importance of NGOs and members of civil society as active participants in global summits. Issues such as globalization and environmental degradation are not bound by geography or inter-state politics; they transcend these boundaries. Thus, global discourse is often used to stress the scope of the issues as well as the diversity of actors involved.

These and many other groups are "getting connected" as part of larger movements "off-line." What these groups indicate is the various ways in which the Internet is used by groups working on global feminist issues—to gain publicity, to solicit donations, to serve as an educational resource, to create organizational networks. The distinctions in political organization and scope serve as examples of the diversity of ways feminists build coalitions and projects. In addition to using the Internet as a tool within their respective projects, these organizations contribute to the diversity of political movements on-line, currently being articulated as global or international, feminist or humanist, primarily for women or including gender issues. However, what is striking about these groups is that none of them represent the two ends of the spectrum—the "universal sisterhood model" of unity or an antifoundational approach to feminist organizing (à la Butler (1990) or Haraway (1991)). In the next section, we will analyze an emerging on-line trend that holds many possibilities for future articulations of feminist theory and practice.

Feminism Re-defined On-line

One of the most interesting trends on the Net is the abundance of young women who are carving out the space to revision female identity and feminism. Cybergrrls, Webgrrls, and Guerrilla girls are just a few of the groups with a Net presence. For some, the mission is to create a space for women to network and learn how to survive on-line. For others, it is cultural critique. Of interest is how young feminists on-line are imagining future feminisms that may speak to the sorts of coalitions introduced by Butler (1990) or Haraway (1991).

The "3rd WWWave" is an example of these "grrl" groups. They are especially relevant to this discussion because they state that they are concerned with finding "solutions for a more woman-friendly world." According to the website, 3rd WWWave is "a group of women who feel passionately about women's issues, and [have] decided to put up a site that would reflect the unique view of women's issues and feminism in the generation of women who came of age in the '80s. They state that "[f]eminism is not dead; in fact, it's on the rise again, but in a new form."[22] The 3rd WWWave is primarily a response to second-wave feminism, which they juxtapose to their vision. According to the 3rd WWWave, the issues have changed. For instance, feminism is not about breaking the glass ceiling, but rather "leaving the building and climbing up to the roof." It is not about freedom from the chains of marriage but the ability to create positive, heterosexual marriages (among other options). And it is not about "breaking the silence about rape and sexual abuse," but "breaking the silence about consensual sex."[23] The tone regarding the differences between second and 3rd WWWave vary from defensive and confrontational—"we've had enough—and we're doing something about it"—to images of simply passing the torch—"we are building on what [2nd wave feminists] have accomplished."[23]

According to the 3rd WWWave, they "want to be part of the Women's Movement that seeks to empower women all over the world, to question the rigid gender roles we live with, and to generally make women and girls feel like their opinions, values, and dreams matter."[24] However, in their focus on the differences between 2nd and 3rd WWWave feminists, they ignore the differences between the women they claim to represent. The "we" of the 3rd WWWave is assumed, whether that be "we" on the basis of biology, "we" on the basis of generation, or "we" on the basis of common experience and vision. The issues of relevance include work, money, sex, and family, and their vision is based on a liberal feminist call to grant women the same choices and freedoms as men. In addition, they react to radical feminist arguments that heterosexual sex and marriage are inherently oppressive to women. While they claim to be speaking for all women (and men), the scope of the issues are not global, not concerned with issues of race or class, and ironically end up looking much like the mainstream feminism of the second wave—middle class, white, and American. While the 3rd WWWave states that they are concerned with the condition of women around the world, there is a conceptual silence about the differences between women around the world. Thus, the 3rd WWWave sounds much like the "universal sisterhood" model critiqued within feminist thought.

While I am encouraged that young feminists like the 3rd WWWave are adopting the feminist label, it concerns me that they are seemingly unaware of the extensive critiques leveled at second-wave feminists or the "universal sisterhood" model of feminism. In conceptualizing feminist futures, the lessons and mistakes of feminist theory are either ignored, never read, or forgotten. Is it possible that in the space of the Internet, the feminist wheel will be reinvented—from the struggle to add women in, to a questioning of gender identity altogether? For Faith Wilding (2000), this is an example of what she calls the "cycles of feminism." However, she argues that, "[i]f cyberfeminists wish to avoid making the mistakes of past feminists, it behooves them to know and analyze feminist histories very carefully." In negotiating feminism and the Internet, it seems imperative to have strong feminist voices re-articulating where feminism has been, what is currently being debated, what the interconnections are between gender and other oppressions, and how to connect on-line experiences to politics, and to feminist struggles off-line.

While this critique is important, it is also necessary to consider what sorts of possibilities may be articulated by groups like 3rd WWWave. Wilding (2000) argues that "[b]eing bad grrrls on the Internet is not going to change matters much either, nor challenge the status quo, though it may provide refreshing moments of iconoclastic delirium. But if grrrl energy and invention were to be coupled with engaged political savvy and practice.... Imagine!" Imagine, if feminist politics and future visions could engage with the power of Butler's (1990) parodic repetition? Imagine if Haraway's (1991) infidel heteroglossia could be formed on-line? What are the ramifications of feminism being defined as " … anything you want it to be?"[25] While this conception of feminism may seem like a way to avoid contentious definitions which inevitably leave someone/something out, it may also lead to feminism encompassing every-thing, and nothing. As well, are we really able to be anything we want in cyberspace? And will this translate into realities off-line? Perhaps it is with all of these questions in mind that alternative global feminist coalitions can be imagined and built.

Since feminism in cyberspace is in its infancy, these are the questions that must be kept in mind when thinking and acting on-line. Is the Internet a space that lends itself to coalitions "of the moment"? Can feminists on-line connect with global feminist projects off-line? For Wilding,

> While there is a great deal of all kinds of information about feminism available on the Net—and new sites are opening up all the time—it must be remembered that the more this information can be contextualized politically, and linked to practices, activism, and conditions of every day life, the more it is likely to be effective in helping to connect and mobilize people. (2000)

When using the Internet, feminists must keep in mind the reality that people's lives do not begin or end on-line, and therefore, connections must be maintained between these spaces.

Conclusion

The three models of global feminism discussed—universal sisterhood, add difference and stir, and the social movement coalition—represent various forms that global feminist projects take. From this analysis, it is clear that the last two models respond to critiques from women marginalized by the universal sisterhood model of global feminism. While the first two remain committed to identity politics, and are therefore open to many critiques stemming from the difference debate, the social movement coalition model has the most promise of facilitating projects beyond the confines of identity. However, while these three models are representative of political projects both on and off-line, they do not represent postmodern articulations of global feminism, such as Butler's "antifoundational coalitions."

My analysis of these online women's groups indicates that these "global feminist" organizations fit within the add difference and stir model of global feminism—a sign that the debates over difference have had an impact throughout feminist movements, but that gender issues remain prioritized over all others. Valentine M. Moghadam confirms this and states that most articulations of global feminism "are situated in the tradition of progressive modernist politics, rather than in any new wave of postmodernist or identity politics."[26] Feminists must consider moving from an agenda of identity politics based on idealistic notions of a global feminism rooted in universal sex/gender difference to global feminisms which struggle to make links that are politically savvy and responsive to lived experience. This conception of postmodern feminism does not negate commonalities, but neither does it consider them immutable, fixed, or essential. Therefore, in practicing global feminisms, we cannot know ahead of time how our interactions will play out. It is through this indeterminancy, contradiction, and transgression that political possibilities are fostered.

Since the Internet is a space where more and more people go for information, there need to be strong feminist voices, thoughts, and visions on-line. Coalitions which address the effects of global processes and power (including Internet technology) on women's lives have the ability to share information and political strategies, respond in "real-time" to urgent actions, and build campaigns. Feminisms on the edge of the new millennium become visible in yet another cultural space and continue the process of dialogue, debate, revision, and imagination. There is no final word on what place the Internet has for feminism, how feminists will use the Internet as a tool in various projects, or as a space to continue thinking and acting. What is clearer are the tensions within these projects and the questions that remain. How much space is there for activism on the Net when consumerism and entertainment seem to be the main attraction? How do feminists on-line negotiate their privileged position in relation to women who do not even have access to a phone line? How do feminists address the fact that it is because of the underpaid take home-work of "third world women" in the Silicon Valley that

Krista Hunt

there are computers through which Internet activism is possible?[27] How do we channel the energy and commitment of groups like 3rd WWWave with the achievements and experience of feminisms past? What kinds of coalitions will be built through on-line connections? These questions remain, as do the possibilities.

I would like to thank Michael Alex, Michael Dartnell, Christine Saulnier, Melanie Stewart Millar, and Leah Vosko for their helpful comments and suggestions and their tireless support and encouragement. I would also like to acknowledge the financial support of my doctoral research from the Social Science and Humanities Research Council of Canada. Please feel free to contact me at krista@yorku.ca.

[1]Liberal feminists argue that women are equal to men and therefore should be treated as such. This includes having the same legal rights and freedoms, education, and opportunities as men.

[2]The focus of radical feminism is the "root" of women's oppression—sexism, patriarchy, male dominance—and the goal of the movement is to "uproot" it. Thus, radical feminism is a revolutionary movement created by women for women. According to Robyn Rowland and Renate D. Klein, "[t]he first and fundamental theme is that women as a social group are oppressed by men as a social group and that this oppression is the primary oppression for women," see "Radical Feminism: Critique and Construct," *Feminist Knowledge* (New York and London: Routledge, 1990) 271-303.

[3]For more on this, see Mohanty (1991).

[4]See Accion Zapatista at http://www.utexas.edu/ftp/student/nave/. For an analysis of the use of the Internet by the Zapatistas, see "Real and Virtual Chiapas: Magic Realism and the Left," by Judith Adler Hellman, www.yorku.ca/org/socreg/hellman.txt.

[5]See the Mobilization for Global Justice website at http://www.a16.org/

[6]The Beijing conference coincided with the increased hype surrounding the Internet and created the impetus for women around the world to connect pre and post Beijing. For information about the role of technology in building a global women's movement, see Gitter (1999).

[7]http://www.igc.org/vsister/

[8]http://www.rawa.org/index.html

[9]Many initiatives are attempting to deal with the small number of women on-line, including groups lobbying for universal access, to photocopying informa-

tion and distributing it through other media. To learn more about issues of access from around the world, see "Global Networking for Change: Experiences from the APC Women's Program" (http://community.web.net/apcwomen/detailed.htm).

[10] As Whaley states, 2/3 of the world's population have never made a telephone call (1996: 230).

[11] Feminist search engines like Femina (http://femina.cybergrrl.com/netscape.htm) and data bases like Aviva (http://www.aviva.org/gropinex.htm#Non-Governmental) are an important example of creating networks and links which make the Internet more accessible.

[12] www.euronet.nl/~fullmoon/womlist/womlist.html, accessed May 31, 2000.

[13] The sources used were taken from research conducted throughout the Spring, 2000.

[14] The way organizations label themselves varies. Some call themselves "women's groups" and others use the term "feminist." The use of "international" and "global" also varies amongst these groups. However, all of these groups either called themselves feminist or were dedicated to feminist issues such as the effects of war on women, women's access to the Internet, the oppression of women in a particular place, or the gendered dimensions of poverty, globalization, or development, and therefore are considered to be contributing to feminist theory and practice. Feminism is defined within this paper as a broad project consisting of diverse (and sometimes contradictory) theoretical and practical manifestations, part of which includes struggles against gender-based oppressions.

[15] www.womenforwomen.org , accessed June 8, 2000.

[16] www.sigi.org/sigi.htm, accessed June 6, 2000.

[17] www.globalsolidarity.npaid.org/coalition.html, accessed on June 9, 2000.

[18] The debates about the use of the term gender instead of women are presented and analyzed by Baden and Goetz (1995). Arguments against using gender include the fear that gender will shift the focus to men, that women's specific oppression will be ignored, that gender will become co-opted and removed from feminism, and that gender is an attack on family values because it leads to theories on the social construction of sex and gender, and the fluidity of sexuality. Also, see O'Leary (1995).

[19] bell hooks discusses the alienation felt by black women from the white, bourgeois, feminist movement in the United States in *Feminist Theory from Margin to Center* (1984: 43-66). Chandra Talpade Mohanty (1991) speaks to the imperialism of western feminism and the construction of third world

women as victims without voices or agency in "Under Western Eyes." Rejections of feminism may stem from experiences of marginalization and oppression within feminism based on a lack of recognition of the differences between women.

[20]For more discussion about the uses of "international" vs. "global," see Peterson and Runyan (1993).

[21]www.globalsolidarity.npaid.org/globalsol2.html#Creating., accessed June 3, 2000.

[22]www.io.com/~wwave/, accessed June 8, 2000.

[23]www.io.com/~wwave/second_third/thennow.html, accessed June 8, 2000.

[24]www.io.com/~wwave/, accessed June 8, 2000.

[25]www.io.com/~wwave/second_third/index.html, accessed June 8, 2000.

[26]Neo-feminism is another grrl group re-defining feminism in similar ways to the 3rd WWWave. See www.neofeminism.com/defined/neofem2.html, accessed June 8, 2000.

[27]More information on this can be found at www.sfbg.com/cgi-bin/goswish, accessed June 2, 2000.

Appendix A

The Global List of Women's Organizations
www.euronet.nl/~fullmoon/womlist/womlist.html

(These sites are listed them in numerical order, starting with the country with the largest number.)

Country:	Women's Organizations with websites:
United States of America	1172
Australia	48
Canada	46
United Kingdom	19
The Netherlands	18
Germany	16
France	13
South Africa	12

Austria	11
Israel	9
Denmark	8
Sweden & Switzerland	7
Ireland	6
Croatia, Japan, & Russia	4
Italy, New Zealand, Norway, & Spain	3
Egypt, Finland, India, Indonesia, Jordan, Pakistan, Philippines, Poland, Romania, Taiwan, & Thailand	2
Benin, Bolivia, Botswana, Chile, Costa Rica, Czech Republic, Ecuador, Estonia, Ethiopia, Gaza Strip, Greece, Hungary, Kenya, Latvia, Lithuania, Mexico, Moldova, Mongolia, Nicaragua, Peru, Portugal, Senegal, Singapore, Singapore, Slovenia, South Korea, Uganda, Ukraine, & Zimbabwe	1

—Valentine M. Moghadam, "International Feminist Network: Collective Action in an Era of Globalization," *International Sociology* 15 (1) (March 2000): 77-8.

References

Alexander, M. Jacqui and Chandra T. Mohanty. "Introduction: Genealogies, Legacies, Movements." *Feminist Genealogies, Colonial Legacies, Democratic Futures*. Eds. M. Jacqui Alexander and Chandra T. Mohanty. New York: Routledge, 1997. xiii-xlii.

Baden, Sally and Anne Marie Goetz. "Who Needs [Sex] When You Can Have [Gender]? Conflicting Discourses on Gender at Beijing." Unpublished manuscript, 1995.

Bulbeck, Chilla. *One World Women's Movement*. London: Pluto Press, 1988.

Butler, Judith. *Gender Trouble: Feminism and the Subversion of Identity*. New York/London: Routledge, 1990.

Calhoun, Cheshire. "Separating Lesbian Theory from Feminist Theory." *Feminist Social Thought: A Reader*, Ed. Diana Tietjens Meyers. New York and London: Routledge, 1997. 199-218.

Gitter, Alice Mastrangelo. "Mapping Women's Global Communication and

Networking." *women@internet*. Ed. Wendy Harcourt. London and New York: Zed, 1999. 91-101.

Haraway, Donna. *Simians, Cyborgs, and Women: The Reinvention of Nature.* New York: Routledge, 1991.

Hellman, Judith Adler "Real and Virtual Chiapas: Magic Realism and the Left." www.yorku.ca/org/socreg/hellman.txt, accessed February 2, 2000.

hooks, bell. *Feminist Theory from Margin to Center*. Boston: Southend, 1984.

hooks, bell. *Ain't I a Woman*. Boston: South End Press, 1981.

Mohanty, Chandra Talpade "Under Western Eyes: Feminist Scholarship and Colonial Discourses." *Third World Women and the Politics of Feminism*. Eds. Chandra Talpade Mohanty, Ann Russo and Lourdes Torres. Bloomington and Indianapolis: Indiana University Press, 1991. 51-80.

O'Leary, Dale. "The Deconstruction of Women." Mimeo, Beijing, 1995.

Peterson, V. Spike and Anne Sisson Runyan. *Global Gender Issues*. Boulder: Westview Press, 1993.

Plant, Sadie. *Zeros + Ones: Digital Women + the New Technoculture*. New York: Doubleday, 1997.

Negroponte, Nicolas. *Being Digital*. New York : Vintage Books, 1996.

Riley, Denise. *Am I That Name?* Minneapolis: University of Minnesota Press, 1988.

Whaley, Patti. "Potential Contributions of Information Technologies to Human Rights." *Women and Performance* 9 (1)(1996): 225-232.

Wilding, Faith. "Where is Feminism in Cyberspace?" www.obn.org/cfundef/faith_def.html, accessed June 8, 2000.

Contributor Notes

Diane Crocker is currently teaching in the Department of Sociology and Criminology at Saint Mary's University in Halifax. A Ph.D. candidate at York University, her dissertation involves the analysis of over 300 Judicial Decisions in cases of violence against wives. She has also conducted research on and written about workplace sexual harassment.

Krista Hunt is a third-year doctoral candidate in the Department of Political Science at York University in Toronto and the recipient of a SSHRC doctoral fellowship. She has presented at the Feminist Graduate Colloquium in 1997 and 1999, as well as organized the 11th Annual Colloquium in 1999. Currently, she is working on her dissertation which explores "global" feminist organizing and the politics of the Internet.

Chris Klassen has done graduate work in Religion and Culture and is currently a Ph.D. candidate in the Women's Studies programme at York University in Toronto. Her research focus is feminist spirituality, contemporary Goddess worship and modern Witchcraft.

Debra Langan completed her Ph.D. at York University, Toronto, in 1998, and is currently an Assistant Professor in the Department of Sociology at York University. She specializes in social psychology, and continues to explore the ways in which ideologies are perpetuated and/or challenged in small group discussions about violence against women.

Michelle Lowry earned her Master's degree in Sociology and Equity Studies in Education at the Ontario Institute for Studies in Education, University of Toronto. She is currently working towards her Ph.D. in Women's Studies at York University in Toronto. Her research area focuses on concepts of citizenship and belonging in Canadian immigration policy, and the ways in which these understandings are gendered. She is also interested in media representations of immigrants and refugees.

Lucy Luccisano is completing her Ph.D. in Sociology at York University in Toronto. Her work examines the impact of globalization and neo-liberal reforms on social policy and anti-poverty programs in Mexico. Her M.A. research explored social movements in Latin America with a particular focus on Peru.

Melanie Stewart Millar is a doctoral candidate in the Graduate Programme in Political Science at York University in Toronto. She holds an M.A. in Women's Studies (York University), a B.A. in Political Science (University of Victoria). Her recent book, *Cracking the Gender Code: Who Rules the Wired World?* (Toronto: Second Story Press, 1998; Annandale, Australia: Pluto Press, 2000) explores the politics of digital culture and the effects of digital technologies on women. She is currently researching and writing her dissertation on the politics of domestic technology in North America since the 1970s.

Christine Saulnier is originally from Richibucto, New Brunswick. She is a doctoral candidate in Political Science at York University in Toronto. She holds both an M.A. and B.Soc.Sc. in Political Science from the University of Victoria and the University of Ottawa respectively. Her M.A. thesis examined feminist discourse and the politics of new reproductive and genetic technologies in Canada. She is currently writing her Ph.D.dissertation, which examines the gendered politics of health care reform in New Brunswick.

Joanne H. Wright is currently a postdoctoral fellow in the Department of Political Science at Rutgers University. Her postdoctoral research investigates the representations of consent and sexual violence in public discourse and in feminist theory. She holds a Ph.D. in Political Science from York University.

Praise for *Feminism(s) on the Edge of the Millennium:*

This is a wonderful collection of essays that represents the breadth and depth of feminist research being produced by a new generation of scholars. Whether considering women's relationship to technology, women's organizational strategies for change, representations of "women" in classical, Biblical and popular cultural texts, or women's experiences with violence, the volume's essays blend sophisticated theoretical analyses with a clear commitment to making feminist research relevant to women's activism and political change. As the introductory article by editors Hunt and Saulnier make clear, the contributors to the volume all explore the binary opposites (like public/private or practical/strategic) that continue to shape discourses of gender: likewise, the authors seek to challenge the "boundaries created by dominant discourses, thus opening space for alternative conceptualizations of society's problems and solutions." Elegantly written, well-researched, and politically engaged, this volume of essays makes a provocative and important contribution to feminist scholarship, and is an excellent new resource for undergraduate classes.
—Kathryn McPherson, Director, Undergraduate Programmes, School of Women's Studies, York University, Toronto

Feminism(s) on the Edge of the Millennium is a highly enjoyable glimpse into the feminist scholarship of the future. This collection will make a wonderful introduction, for senior undergraduates and the interested reader alike, to new feminist analyses of a wide variety of issues in a number of areas (politics, history, law, sociology, philosophy). The discussions range from communal kitchens to Martha Stewart, from Plato's philosophy of reproduction to the Internet, from goddess worship to the politics of the veil. Taken together, the authors make it clear that, contrary to popular opinion, new feminist scholars are not sequestered in the ivory tower, or engaged in theory for theory's sake, but that they are passionately engaged with the politics of the everyday, analyzing new and old issues alike in informed and thought-provoking ways. The authors challenge traditional feminist concepts and theories with a keen eye for universalisms and essentialisms. They do not, however, discard the feminisms of the past, rather they push feminism forward into new areas of concern and onto new paths for political struggle.
—Leslie Jeffrey, Dept. of History and Politics, University of New Brunswick, Saint John

This book contains a decidedly presumptuous, yet definitely appropriate premise. Under the rubric of "feminism(s) on the edge," Hunt and Saulnier adeptly draw together a wide range of scholarship by dynamic, up and coming, women scholars. The contributors are united beyond various York University doctoral programme affiliations by their concerted efforts to enlarge/enliven contemporary feminist theories and practices. While they perceive themselves to be perched on a precarious "critical edge" of the academy, the authors nonetheless self assuredly soar above a variety of "cutting edge" dilemmas. As a result, each chapter is inventive and insightful. Some incisively transcend leading theoretical formulations, while others feature revelations gleaned from highly involved research methodologies. The contributions glide across time and space and over disciplinary boundaries: from political science and women's studies, to law and sociology. As a result, this collection is eclectic, engaging and inspiring. Most importantly, it serves to spur other scholars, new and old, to take flight and explore the innumerable possibilities/potentialties when it comes to feminist research, writing, and organizing.
—Alexandra Dobrowolsky, Dept. of Political Science, Saint Mary's University, Halifax